And Then Came The Angel

Gospel Sermons For Advent/Christmas/Epiphany Cycle A

William B. Kincaid, III,

CSS Publishing Company, Inc., Lima, Ohio

AND THEN CAME THE ANGEL

Scripture quotations are from the *New Revised Standard Version of the Bible*, copyright 1989 by the Division of Christian Education of the National Council of the Churches of Christ in the USA. Used by permission.

The sermon "And Then Came The Angel" first appeared in *Biblical Preaching Journal,* Fall, 1995. It is reprinted here with permission.

Library of Congress Cataloging-in-Publication Data

Kincaid, William B., 1960
    And then came the angel : Gospel sermons for Advent/Christmas/Epiphany, Cycle A / William B. Kincaid III
        p.   cm.
    Includes bibliographical references.
    ISBN 0-7880-1245-2 (alk. paper)
    1. Advent sermons. 2. Christmas sermons. 3. Epiphany season—Sermons. 4. Bible. N.T. Gospels—Sermons. 5. Christian Church (Disciples of Christ)—Sermons. 6. Sermons. I. Title.
BV4254.5.K77   1998
252'.61—dc21
                                                                            98-9384
                                                                            CIP

This book is available in the following formats, listed by ISBN:
    0-7880-1245-2   Book
    0-7880-1246-0   IBM
    0-7880-1247-9   Mac
    0-7880-1248-7   Sermon Prep

PRINTED IN U.S.A.

For my friends at North Middletown

With Love and Thanksgiving

Table Of Contents

Preface

It is clear that people expect different things from sermons. Some want sermons to be entertaining. Others believe that a sermon is nothing more than "a talk" if it does not send half the world to eternal damnation. Those looking for quick and neat answers probably will be frustrated by this collection. Those attracted to this book with the thought that it might shed further light on the popular topic of angels surely will be disappointed.

The sermon is as much an act of worship as any other part of the worship service. It is an offering to God. At the same time, it is yet another opportunity to engage our hearts and minds in the on-going effort of discerning the mind of Jesus Christ. I hope these sermons contribute in some way to that process.

The writing of fourteen sermons did not sound like a daunting task when I agreed to put this collection together. However, the ink was barely dry on the contract when I began to feel a certain amount of discomfort. I attribute this to several things. First, there are so many words thrown around these days that I have some reluctance about adding to the excess. Second, the form of a sermon is not written, but spoken. Something is lost when a sermon is removed from the particular setting in which it is preached and heard. Third, few things create anxiety like putting words on a page for others to see and read and critique.

Finally, and most importantly, some of the ideas in these sermons continue to cause me discomfort. Part of the challenge of preaching is to hold out a vision of what God's world should look like, even though most of us still are struggling with implementing that vision in our own lives. As much as I want you to be comforted and encouraged by these sermons, I hope you will feel some of the discomfort that I believe these lessons heap upon us. The gospel of Jesus Christ is both comforting and challenging.

Most of these sermons were preached while I was the minister of the North Middletown Christian Church (Disciples of Christ). I enjoyed my ministry there immensely and always will be grateful for the love and support the people of that congregation gave to me. Not only did they extend constant encouragement to their minister, they shared in the ministry of the church in an extraordinary way. People all along the way have shaped me as a person and as a minister. I would not want to miss this opportunity to thank all of you.

How Unexpected Can Christmas Be?

Matthew 24:36-44

The temptation is to dismiss these words from Matthew. After all, how do they pertain to us? Written at a time when the early church had bet its life on Jesus' return, these seem odd words to hear on the first Sunday of Advent. We are busy preparing the crèche for a baby, but Matthew appears to be announcing Jesus' second coming. And it isn't just an odd lesson, but a frightening one. In a season when we seek assurance, Matthew's words are enough to scare us half to death. These words compare the coming of God's promised one to the death and devastation of the flood during Noah's time. We are looking forward to being reunited with family and friends while this lesson speaks of untimely separation and unpredictable departure. And then, in the event our Advent and Christmas sensibilities are not offended completely, the coming of Jesus is compared to a thief who breaks into a house at an unexpected hour. Matthew doesn't know much about the holidays.

It is for these reasons that dismissing this passage would be an easy task. Yet, the church includes this lesson or one like it on the first Sunday of Advent of every year. It isn't just Matthew who thinks these are timely and important words. By including this as a lectionary text the church has agreed with the gospel writer. Before we get too far into December, before any significant plans are made about our Advent celebration, the wisdom of the saints dictates that we read this passage from Matthew.

Perhaps it has something to do with this theme of preparation. "Get ready, people," the Lord says, "because I haven't even let the angels in on the secret. I may come at the least expected time. Be prepared!" We appreciate the advice, but we have been getting ready for this season since about this time last year. We bought our wrapping paper the week after Christmas last December. We have picked up gifts throughout the year as we have come across certain unique items that we might not be able to find anywhere else. One strand of Christmas lights was so hard to take down that we decided to leave it up year around. What more preparation could we make?

With an economic landscape that ranges from New York City advertising firms to strip malls anchored by Wal-Mart stores, businesses are making sure we are prepared. It is clear we are still in danger of spending more time at the mall than at the manger, but even these places help us get ready. Before the plastic pumpkins and black capes of Halloween are put away, hints of Christmas are seen in displays here and there. By mid-November shoppers have to step over artificial poinsettias on their way to their favorite department. Called the biggest shopping day of the year, the Friday after Thanksgiving is not for the faint of heart. Christmas trees start standing up in living rooms and sanctuaries alike. Advent wreaths are aglow with promise and light. We attend special services. Greeting cards from loved ones, complete with quotes from scripture, are taped to the mantle with care. We don't want to be too hard on Matthew, especially since the gospel writer did not have two thousand years worth of tradition to draw upon, but we have lots of preparation for Christmas.

Don't you see why it would be so easy to send this lesson into the same scriptural oblivion where we send other Bible passages that we have deemed irrelevant and archaic? Like so many other parts of scripture which seem to fit better with first century Palestine, this is a tough passage for reasonable, intelligent people to take seriously. The frightening words appear to be a poor match for the assurance of Advent. The urgency is lost on a world that does not seem to change much from year to year. As for Matthew's insistence that we be prepared, most of us are more than ready for Christmas to be over with by the time it gets here. You see, the cat is out of the bag. For us, Christmas comes on December 25. That has not always been the date for the celebration of Jesus' birth, but it has been for the last fifteen hundred years. We know Matthew says that not even the angels in heaven know the hour, but it appears that they are the only ones! The rest of us know. It is December 25. It's that date every year, and there is nothing that is even remotely unexpected about it. How could there be?

With this date securely determined, with all the help we have in getting ready, even the late afternoon, Christmas Eve shoppers have no excuse. Yet, in convincing ourselves that we are ready, or at least that we will be ready when time draws closer, there is for some of us this nagging emptiness. Maybe it is the rush of it all. Maybe it is fighting the traffic. Maybe it is the sense of obligation too many gift-givers feel. Maybe it is the financial over-extension which adds pressure to the late-winter months.

For whatever reason, we may find that we are not as prepared as we once thought. Matthew may have been on to something after all. Perhaps it is time to reconsider what it means to be prepared. There is this possibility that being prepared for Christmas means more than finishing our shopping. Advent and Christmas are compromised badly when we focus too much on what is under the tree and too little on who is in the stable. The coming of Christmas is not the same thing as the coming of the Lord.[1] It may have been once upon a time, but it's not anymore. "Are you ready for Christmas" asks a different question from "Are you ready for the Lord?" Of course, we are ready for Christmas. With this much notice, everybody ought to be ready for Christmas. "Are you ready for Jesus?" Now, that's a different question.

We have allowed the early Christmas displays to lure us into a false sense of readiness. We have fallen prey to advertisements and commercials that tell us our level of preparation can be measured by whether we have purchased their product for our friend or spouse or child. Even in church, we are led to believe if we light a few candles and bring out the greenery we are somehow ready for Christmas. Well, we may be ready for Christmas, or at least what Christmas has become, but that is not the same thing as being receptive to the presence of God living at the center of our lives.

But hear this: Outlandish ads and outlet malls do not determine the time or the content or the nature of what is at the heart of this celebration. It is not Christmas until God says it is Christmas.

The first Christmas happened to coincide with the coming of the Lord. God longs for that to be at the heart of our celebration again. Most of us have tried the commercial side of this holiday and found it to be wanting. We too want our Christmas to coincide with the coming of the Lord. We want that Light to shine into our lives, to illuminate our homes, to dispel the darkness in our world. We want to anchor our lives in that baby named Jesus, to be loved as we have never been loved, to focus our lives on the lasting and important things. We want that Messiah to eradicate evil and eliminate poverty and ease human suffering. We want that voice to stand up for the poor and stand against oppressive powers and stand among the hurting of the world.

Let's be clear about what we are talking about when we refer to "the coming of the Lord." Some are holding out for Jesus to arrive a second time by riding in on a cloud. Some spend so much time speculating about that possibility that they give insufficient consideration to Jesus' first visit. The coming of the Lord in this Advent season has to do with how this story of God-with-us continues to demand our attention and allegiance. The issue is not how God may be revealed at some later point, but how we respond to the way God was revealed at the birth of Jesus. The Word has become flesh and in seasons like this one we focus more intently on what that means for our lives.

The question haunts us. "Are you ready for that kind of Christmas?" To be ready for Christmas in the biblical story does not involve relaxation, but upheaval. We know that the coming of the Lord will challenge priorities and prejudices. We know that the kind of world for which we long cannot be accomplished without confrontation and change. We know that kind of messiah, no doubt, will ask a lot of us. Are we ready for that kind of Christmas?

It is interesting what we have done to this concept of messiah. From time to time we hear people practically making sport of those who were unable to recognize Jesus because he came into the world as a helpless baby. That is, after all, the way a large percentage of us come into the world. There's some question how much anticipation there was for the coming of the messiah. For those who were looking for a messiah, it is usually assumed that they were looking in political palaces and courts of honor and homes of wealth. Our messiah, of course, slipped in the back door through the unlikely entrance of a stable, accompanied by poor parents and smelly animals. It is true that many were so certain of the circumstances of the messiah's birth that they were not able to recognize anything which contradicted their own thinking. That reminds us that we cannot pin down God. This doing-a-new-thing God of ours is full of surprises.

However, in one respect, we are the ones who have missed the point. The hope for a messiah in the Old Testament is a hope for a political figure who would set things right. Part of the reason the people ached for a messiah was because the world was in such a sad shape. A baby, even one named Jesus, was dismissed from consideration because a baby could not bring about the changes that were so desperately needed. And whoever heard of a carpenter from Nazareth becoming the messiah? Then and now, carpenters were useful people, but they did not have the power to correct the injustices.

Hungry people were being ignored. Poor people were being neglected. Sick people were being forgotten. Those who were different were being left out. People of all kinds were yearning for a center to their lives that would bring more hope and meaning than they had been able to find elsewhere.

Today, hungry people are equated with being lazy. City highways are designed to take traffic over and around the out-of-sight, out-of-mind poor. Neighborhoods are closing their hearts and doors to centers where AIDS patients can spend their final days in dignity. And people of all kinds are still yearning for a center to their lives that will bring more hope and meaning than we have been able to find elsewhere.

It will be easier to celebrate Christmas than to celebrate the coming of the Lord. We know that the coming of the Lord into our lives, churches, and communities will mean change. We have made Jesus into an object of personal devotion, but the mission of the messiah was much broader. The messiah was to be a political figure who would establish God's ways as the rule for humankind.[2] The messiah did not come to bless our prejudices and to look the other way from our indiscretions. No, the messiah came to lift up the humble and bring down the proud, to call people away from division and into community, to calm fears and instill courage, and to evoke our compassion for the hurting and left-out of the world. And we know changes like that are going to be painful because most of us have something invested in keeping things as they are.

Christmas has a comfortable ring to it, but the coming of the Lord stretches and pulls and gnaws at us. Christmas will allow for family gatherings by the fireplace, but the coming of the Lord will call us to see every person on the planet as part of the family. Christmas will save us from the messiness of a troubled world; the coming of the Lord will save us from ourselves and push us to transform the messiness so that we can have real peace with ourselves and each other.

As it turns out, Matthew was right. We know that a loving God does not want pain and sorrow to continue. We do not know the hour or the day, but we shouldn't be too surprised if some voice calls us to an even greater generosity on behalf of the suffering of the world. We shouldn't be too taken aback if we are tapped on the shoulder and directed toward some worthwhile community project that needs our support. We shouldn't be too startled if we begin noticing things that just aren't right and go to work to change them to benefit other people. We shouldn't be too alarmed if we find ourselves being led to develop a deeper spiritual center for our lives.

It could happen at anytime. Some will respond, some won't. That's okay. At some later point, some other unexpected hour, they too may respond. The good news is that we are sure God isn't going to give up on us. God does not forget or forsake. God comes to us. For some, God brings renewed promises that they are loved. From some, God requires evidence that kind of love is still real and alive in the world. For whatever our part will be, we are asked only to be ready.

———————

1. Fred Craddock, et al., *Preaching Through the Christian Year A* (Philadelphia: Trinity Press International, 1992), p. 9.

2. Paul J. Achtemeier, General Editor, *Harper's Bible Dictionary* (San Francisco: Harper, 1985), p. 630.

Speak For Yourself!

Matthew 3:1-12

What do Richard Nixon and Shirley Temple have in common? While they may have shared many common interests and traits, isn't it true that neither one ever outlived their pasts? When Richard Nixon was buried behind the house that his father built, he went to his grave as the president that was forced to resign in the face of humiliation and scandal. Even amid his remarkable rehabilitation which included significant contributions to the world's conversation about public policy, Nixon may as well have had "Watergate" stamped on his forehead. He never outlived a disgraceful past.

The same is true with Shirley Temple, only in a different way. Shirley Temple sang and danced her way into the hearts of the world as a little girl with blonde curly hair. She lifted spirits, inspired generations of performers, and made people feel good about themselves. She was nothing short of a blessing, but to this day, despite a number of other accomplishments and contributions, she is remembered as a little girl with blonde, curly hair. Shirley Temple's past is wonderful, but she will never outlive that past.

It is very difficult to put away our pasts, and that goes as much for us as it does for people of public notoriety. Most all of us can think of some decision that we made that turned out to be the wrong decision, some situation that now we wish we had handled differently, or some act that we committed that we would never do again if we had the chance to live that part of our lives over. A man wakes up seven weeks into a new marriage and realizes he has married the wrong person. A woman invests 25 years in a career that she never really enjoyed, but now she fears it is too late to start over. A family who always wanted to enjoy the benefits of the city never got around to moving and now clouds of regret hang over their every gathering.

If there is something bad in our past, and there surely is in everybody's past, that is a high hurdle to jump. Near the end of every governor's term he or she may choose to grant pardons for certain criminals. These pardons may restore some civil rights, but not all of them. Even with some privileges restored and their debts to society paid, those people will spend the rest of their days trying to outlive the bad things in their pasts.

We know that convicted felons aren't the only ones who struggle to put past mistakes behind them. There may not have been any charges filed, but the girl who caused the wreck that killed the innocent people always will have to contend with those memories. The man may have lost control only once, but the memory of his open hand on his wife's face will haunt him as long as he lives. It is hard to put our pasts behind us.

Some bad things are well known and the news makes the rounds all too quickly. Some bad things are words and deeds and thoughts known only to us. The fact that our mistakes are lesser known does not make them less serious. As Tony Campolo says, "We need to be saved from those things about ourselves that would cause us to hate ourselves." Sometimes we are harder on ourselves than we need to be. Sometimes the people around us are not nearly as tolerant as they should be. Whatever the situation, it is hard to put away a past that has some glaring flaw in it. Yet, there is good news. God loves us. God forgives us. God longs for us to come to grips with whatever it is that is keeping us from full communion with God.

Sometimes we have made no mistake, but some visit from tragedy's storehouse has left us sad and angry and bitter. We can't explain some of the diseases, but we know what they have done to our lives. We are left without the ones we love and with a gaping hole in our lives. One man was accused falsely of raping a family member's friend. He was the victim of a sick world where people allege all sorts of things which never happened anywhere except in their own imagination. That man has experienced enormous pain, yet he made no mistake.

Nobel Peace Prize winner Elie Wiesel has written over thirty books. Each one has been informed and shaped by his experience as a Holocaust survivor. They are powerful, moving books which merit our reading, but surely they are as much therapy for him as they are information for us. Wiesel's only crime was being born a Jew, but that alone forced him to watch family members and friends be tortured and killed. Yet, there is good news, even in those cases where we are not responsible for the pain in our past. We may never get over some things, but we can learn to live with them. God will be present as we begin to heal bit by bit. God will be the fellow traveler as we rise and continue the journey.

If you don't have anything in your past that is bad, if there isn't anything that you need to work through, then praise God, give thanks, and look out! Sometimes dealing with a good past is the most difficult task of all. A part of this passage is for those of us who can't think of any mistake or flaw or regret. People who can't think of any bad in their pasts are people who quickly lose sight of their need for God. It is easy to reach a comfort level where we convince ourselves that we already know what we need to know. Sermons become a form of entertainment or conversation starters, rather than a discussion about applying the words of scripture to our daily lives. It is easy to come to church because we enjoy it instead of coming because we need to be here. At one church's general assembly, which happened to coincide with the World Series, some people entered the sanctuary wearing headphones so they could listen to the game during worship. Such is life in the comfort zone — scripture is intended for somebody else because we have heard it all before. In the comfort zone we can relax and draw upon the spiritual capital we have accumulated through the years.[1] A good past is hard to overcome.

On the television show *M*A*S*H*, Dr. Charles Emerson Winchester III made it clear what separated him from everybody else. "I'm a Winchester," he was heard to say more than once. For him, it was his family name that made him superior to everyone else. Other people carry other burdens. One woman received her education at Harvard and found a way to work Harvard into every conversation. Congregations fall victim to the same problem. Churches become satisfied with their pasts to the point that they do not make the changes necessary to live in the present with the same degree of faithfulness shown in prior years. It's one thing to be proud of certain things, but it is possible to lean too heavily on a good past and live too scantily in the precious present.

In the great hymn "There's A Wideness In God's Mercy," there is the most wonderful phrase. One verse begins with good news for people trying to deal with some mistake in a bad past. "There is welcome for the sinner," the verse begins. To know that we are welcome to come back is often what leads us to come back. To experience that welcome, at home or church or work or among friends, prompts tears of joy. But then hear how that line continues. "There is welcome for the sinner, and more graces for the good." Those of us who think we are on the right track are the people who need that double dose of grace. We are the ones who depend too much on ourselves and lean too heavily on our own accomplishments. The people who have to deal with a strong and rich past need more grace, not less. We have to be convinced ever so gently of our need and then nurtured toward making God our center instead of making our center god.

That's what John the Baptist was dealing with in this lesson. In scripture's continuing assault on the religious people of the day, John the Baptist was completely unimpressed with the very thing that the Jewish people had built their lives upon. For the Jewish people, Abraham was more than a special ancestor. Abraham's life and faith had made provision for everybody who followed Abraham in the faith, even those who came along many generations later. To the "children of Abraham" belonged the favor of God, and the favor of God would never be taken from them.

Then comes John the Baptist. He tells them that just because they are children of Abraham doesn't mean that the requirements have been eased or that they can slack off. We hate to hear John the Baptist say that because we know how it translates to our situation.[2] We can hear him now. "Just because you are members of the church, just because you give your weekly offerings, just because your great-grandparents were in this church, just because you are an officer, just because you are the minister, doesn't mean it is time to relax and take it easy and give in to this temptation of thinking this matter of being Christian is under control." In other words, don't presume your past has taken care of your present. Don't presume either way. Don't presume that your life is over if you have something bad in your past. Don't presume, either, that a good past is permission to relax.

The call to repent, to turn toward God, is for all of us to hear, and for us to hear over and over again. Wasn't it John's concern that people were taking their faith for granted, experiencing it secondhand through Abraham, and coasting in automatic pilot? And shouldn't that be our concern? There is more to see and hear and experience than we have seen and heard and experienced! Every day requires a renewed commitment to God, an increased awareness of God, and a greater participation in the ways of God. Every day calls us to engage our lives with the spirit of God. Others will contribute to our growth and understanding, and we will learn some things from our pasts, but responsibility falls on us to respond to the presence of the living God every day in a way that deepens our faith.

A friend tells of the Saturdays he spent going to football games with his father. The boy and his dad sat in sunshine and rain, wind and snow, and cheered for their favorite team. There was nothing like it. On the way home from the ball games, prior to the era of drive-through windows, they often stopped to get a bite to eat. The boy would stand at the counter and listen to his father give the order for their food. Sometimes the restaurant person would turn to the boy and ask, "And what for you today?" It was very comforting for the boy to point to his father and say, "I'm with him." Those were the days. The boy's father took care of everything and all the boy had to do was stand there and wait on his food. If anybody happened to ask, he could always say, "I'm with him."

At some point, we start answering for ourselves. It is frightening at first, and sometimes it is still frightening years later, but the call to repent is a call each person must answer for him or herself. The fact that we answered that call once doesn't answer for us today. It is not a matter of having to prove ourselves over and over, but a matter of daily confessing that we stand in constant need of the strength and grace of God.

When Jesus asked the disciples, "Who do you say that I am?" it was a pointed question aimed at each person. Jesus didn't ask, "Who did your grandparents say that I am?" The question was not, "Who does your church say that I am?" It wasn't even, "Once upon a time, who did you say that I am?" The question is present tense. "Who do you say that I am?"

Who do you say that I am? Isaiah responded, "Wonderful Counselor, Mighty God, Everlasting Father, Prince of Peace" (Isaiah 9:6).

Who do you say that I am? Simon Peter answered, "You are the Christ, the Son of the living God" (Matthew 16:16).

Who do you say that I am? John of Patmos said, "King of kings and Lord of lords" (Revelation 19:16).

This very day, regardless of what is in the past, Jesus asks, "Who do you say that I am?" This is our chance to speak for ourselves, to claim the faith, to experience the nearness of the kingdom firsthand, and to live our answer every day of our lives.

---

1. William Barclay, *The Gospel of Matthew,* Volume 1, Revised Edition (Philadelphia: Westminster Press, 1975), p. 47.

2. Douglas R.A. Hare, *Matthew* (Louisville: John Knox Press, 1993), p. 20.

Room For Questions

Matthew 11:2-11

It's interesting how we fix in our minds certain images of people and block other images of the same people. We do that to biblical characters. We remember Peter's denial of Jesus, but forget his powerful preaching recorded in the book of Acts. Or, we remember how women came to Jesus for help from time to time, but forget how Jesus depended on the women for financial support and to announce the news of the resurrection. We remember David's tryst with Bathsheba, but forget his courage and leadership in other instances. The temptation, especially in a culture that conditions us to remember the worst about people, is to remember the mistakes and forget the moments of brilliance.

Sometimes it's the other way around. Sometimes we remember the good moments of a person's life and gladly forget the unseemly events. Perhaps what we should remember is that we are all more complex than a single decision, or a single position on an issue, or a single event. It is wasted time to judge anyway, but especially so if we are only going to consider one moment out of a person's life. All of us are better than our worst moments. All of us are people with winding journeys and interesting stories, and none of us ought to be labeled for life as the result of only one scene from our lives.

We shouldn't do that to the people around us, and we shouldn't do that to the biblical characters either. Look at John the Baptist. What do we remember about John the Baptist? We recall him preaching in the wilderness, calling people to repent of their sins and awaken to the kingdom of heaven. We recall his clothing and his diet. It's not every preacher that wears a suit made of camel's hair, and very few limit their caloric intake to locusts and wild honey. We even remember his turning up the heat on the Pharisees and Sadducees, calling them a "brood of vipers." What a wonderful picture we have of John the Baptist — confident, courageous, intense, and enthusiastic! Someone decisive and certain was needed to announce the coming of Jesus, and John was just that person. That's how we remember the Baptizer. Any other description would be difficult to recognize.

Then we encounter this story from Matthew. It shows John the Baptist in a light so different that we would swear it is not the same person. Now John the Baptist is in jail, but that's not all of it. A question is on his lips, one that we can barely believe he is asking. John is inquiring about the identity of Jesus. Of all people, we thought John the Baptist knew more about Jesus than anybody. But here John is sending his disciples to ask Jesus, "Are you the one who is to come, or are we to wait for another?" What happened to the decisiveness, the certainty? What happened to his courageous and enthusiastic convictions? Did John the Baptist not know for sure if Jesus was the messiah?

What we should realize is that this is as much a part of John's life as any other part. We all have had moments of decisive commitments and unbounded energy, as well as times of deep uncertainty and extreme tentativeness. John was about to be beheaded because of a king granting a frivolous request at a dinner party. The time was ripe for looking back, tying up loose ends, and reflecting on how he had spent his life. We have been there, or have seen others there. It doesn't happen only at the end of one's life, but all along the way we wonder if that decision was best, or that stance was right, or that choice appropriate.

Maybe life in a jail cell was wearing on him. Maybe Jesus was so different from what John expected that he wondered if Jesus could really be the messiah. Maybe John was doubting his earlier convictions. Maybe John wanted the chance to look elsewhere if Jesus was not the messiah. We could speculate endlessly about what brought on the change in John the Baptist, but our time would be better spent thinking about John's question. "Are you the one," he asked of Jesus, "or should we wait for another?"

We feel bad about asking, but we need to know, just as John the Baptist needed to know. We aren't likely to place our trust completely in anyone, or forsake all the other options, or give up all we have, if Jesus is not the one we think he is. "Jesus, are you the one?"

That is the kind of question that can get people in trouble. In some churches and homes, questions aren't very welcome. They are the last thing that some people want to hear. Even in some churches who for years have prided themselves on granting to every individual the freedom to ask questions, the tide has turned. In a number of churches there is no room for questions anymore, only answers. Those answers come with an authority that demands total allegiance and makes no allowance for possible differences in interpretation.

"Are we really sure what Jesus would have thought about abortion and capital punishment and welfare?" "Is there salvation in other religions?" "What did Paul mean when he talked about the role of women in the church?" "Why do bad things happen to good people?" Those questions, legitimate as they may seem, are out of bounds in many churches. Instead of a freedom to explore and grow in the faith, people are given a list of beliefs which eliminates all the questions. Often those who hand out the answers do so in a way that makes people feel guilty if they ever choose to believe differently.

In many homes questions are frowned upon. The attitude expressed by a number of parents is, "I'll tell you the things you need to know when you need to know them." It is a way of keeping insecure parents in control of a situation. Again, life becomes a set of easy, neat answers. However, children soon learn that those easy, neat answers don't provide much of a foundation for living in a hard, complex world. And despite the best efforts of parents to squelch their children's questions, they still ask them. "What is happening to my body?" "Why are people starving in the world when we throw food out every night?" "If people are homeless, why can't they come and sleep in one of our spare bedrooms?" "Why can't I date that person?"

Questions can cause discomfort. In the church they often are seen as a sign of someone's losing faith or causing trouble. In homes they are considered signs of promiscuity. Most of the time, they are neither. They are simply questions. They are the cries of people who have found the easy answers to be empty. They are the yearnings of people who have found the neat answers to be inadequate. Frequently we ask questions as a means of sorting through the options, or gaining firsthand knowledge of something, or of becoming separate individuals. After all, at some point we need to know for ourselves. We may find that our discoveries are different from those of our parents, teachers, and ministers, or we may find that they are fairly similar, but every person needs and deserves the right to become one's own person. Without the freedom to ask questions, without the freedom to arrive at answers different from the ones given to us by others, we do not grow in our own understanding of anything.

Eugene Peterson, a Presbyterian minister who teaches at Regent College in Vancouver, tells the story of wanting to discuss some feelings and energies he was having that he believed had to do with God. It was the summer after Peterson's second year of college. His first two attempts at finding someone who would listen to him didn't work out very well. Peterson tried talking to his pastor, but after about five minutes his pastor diagnosed Peterson's problem as having to do with sex and began a lengthy lecture on the subject. Peterson decided after a couple of meetings that it was his pastor who had a problem with sex, so he began to look elsewhere for someone with whom he could talk about the things he was experiencing and feeling. Then Peterson talked with a man who was considered a saint in his home congregation. This man decided that they should study and discuss Ephesians together, but as it turns out there was no discussion to it. The man simply used Peterson as an audience and lectured endlessly about Ephesians to the young boy.

Finally, Peterson encountered one who treated his God-interest and prayer-hunger with dignity. Instead of trying to shovel Peterson full of pious wisdom or viewing him as a "project," a man named Rueben Lance prayerfully listened to Peterson and all his hopes and fears, questions and feelings. Years later Peterson would write, "He let me be. He didn't mess with my soul. He treated me with dignity. I felt a large roominess in his company — a spiritual roominess, room to move around, room to be free."[1]

Questions aren't bad, but not allowing them to be asked is. Questions are a way of loving God with our minds. Through questions we reach and explore and gain a better understanding of important matters. And even if someone else already has the very same answer, it is still worth the journey for us to come to know it firsthand. Don't be disturbed by John's question, or other people's questions, or by your own. Instead, let us give thanks that our faith is still alive enough to ask questions. Let us give thanks that we haven't succumbed to this notion that we have heard it all before. Let us give thanks for those people in our lives who have created "the roominess" in which we are free to ask and explore and grow and learn. Let us give thanks for people who have opened for us new doors and different ways of thinking. Let us give thanks for people whose acceptance and love toward us was so certain that we found room to move around and be free without the fear of being judged for our questions.

Sometimes asking the right questions is more important than having the right answers. We don't have to live very long before we realize that we no sooner get an answer in our possession before it creates a hundred more questions. What does it mean that God is love? What action does my faith compel me to make in a world of pain and confusion? What else can I learn from this parable? What did this hymn mean to me when I was a child and what does it mean to me now?

Grady Nutt used to tell the story of taking a goldfish out of a bowl and placing it in a large body of water. He said that for several hours the goldfish would continue to swim in little, tiny circles because it had not yet learned of the vastness of the pool. "Are you the one?" John the Baptist asked. Evidence came back to John that suggested Jesus was the one, the messiah, but it was still important for him to ask the question. John must have been asking, "Is he the

27

one for me?" "Do I dare call him my savior and accept all the implications that may bring?"

We who continue to prepare our hearts for the arrival of the Christ-child should find ourselves asking the same question. Most of us said years ago that he is the one, but that was the first step on a journey that lasts a lifetime. We still need to ask our questions as a sign that we are open to the growth and new life that God wills for us all. It is not until we ask, and ask over and over again, that we come to realize what Jesus' being the one means for our lives. There is room to grow in our faith and explore the deep possibilities of our commitment. There is room to swim in the vastness of the pool.

---

1. Eugene H. Peterson, *Under the Unpredictable Plant* (Grand Rapids, Michigan: William B. Eerdmans Publishing Company, 1992,) p. 186.

And Then Came The Angel

Matthew 1:18-25

If we cannot relate to Joseph and appreciate his situation, then our lives are simple, easy lives indeed. Now, by relating to Joseph or understanding what he endured, I don't mean to suggest that we all either have been engaged or married to someone impregnated by the Holy Spirit. Even in our frantic search for ways to explain how such a thing might have happened, we probably didn't think of blaming the Holy Spirit!

We relate to Joseph and appreciate his struggle in a different way, a much more practical way, a day to day sort of way. All of us have had decisions before us about which we have thought and prayed and sought advice. It may have been marriage; it may have been divorce. It may have been choosing a career; it may have been retirement. It may have been surgery; it may have been other treatment.

For Joseph, it was marriage or divorce. And lest that sounds like a simple choice, let us be reminded of the many considerations which are a part of either of these two options. Very few couples, if any, come to the altar with the thought that their marriage might not work. Even fewer come to the altar thinking that divorce is a way out if the marriage does fail. Marriage is an awesome decision and the vast majority of people who get married believe their marriage will last.

Divorce is an equally awesome decision. When a marriage ends, there is almost always one person who is willing to do whatever it takes to save the marriage, and often both people are actively involved in an effort to revive and sustain their marriage. By now, most every family has been touched in some way by divorce, but some still think of it as an easy way out for someone who has grown tired of a relationship. Those who have been through a divorce know that it is one of the most humiliating experiences one can endure. The sense of failure is overwhelming. Years are spent trying to overcome the guilt and second-guessing.

Marriage and divorce are awesome considerations. They are for us, and they were for Joseph. Even though things were different in those days, we can tell from the very delicate way in which Matthew tells this story that this decision for Joseph carried with it huge implications for his future.

Marriage normally had three steps then. First came the engagement in which the marriage partner was selected. This often was done by the families. The second stage was the betrothal which lasted about a year and required total faithfulness to one another. As a matter of fact, in order to break off the betrothal one had to secure a writ of divorce. The third stage was that of marriage to one another, actually living with one another.

It was during that second stage that we find Joseph faced with this monumental decision. It was during the betrothal stage which required complete faithfulness to one another and yet did not permit them to know one another intimately that Joseph found Mary to be with child. And, to be fair, it must have surprised Mary as much as it did Joseph.

Matthew says two things about Joseph. Both of these things made this decision of marriage or divorce that much more difficult. First, Matthew says Joseph was a just and righteous man. More often than not, what that meant in Joseph's society, as in our own, is that a comfortable and safe distance is kept between the righteous people and the unrighteous people. That's not the way it is supposed to be, but that is the way it often is. Parents say to their children, "Don't date that girl," or "Don't run around with that boy." That was the pressure Joseph felt. What would the people say if this good man with a fine reputation continued to be seen with this young woman who was inexplicably pregnant and not yet married?

Matthew also says Joseph was unwilling to expose Mary to public shame. It was not Joseph's desire to disgrace and humiliate Mary. Joseph was sensitive to the horrible ways a divorced, single mother might be treated. Joseph decided that if it must be divorce, he would do so quietly without playing it out for personal benefit or sympathy.

For Joseph, it was marriage or divorce, and what we know about him tells us that this was a very difficult decision. To uphold his reputation in the community, what choice did he have but to divorce this young woman? In order to maintain his family's dignity and honor, he had to distance himself from Mary.

But what about those feelings which he had for Mary? Even in arranged marriages, surely the time spent during their engagement planning their future meant something. And what about the days during their betrothal in which they anxiously awaited the blissful day of their marriage?

At first it may have sounded like an easy option for Joseph— marriage or divorce, but when we begin to weigh all the factors, Joseph's decision was a very difficult one. It doesn't say how long it took Joseph to reach his decision or how many people he asked for advice, but Matthew does say that Joseph decided to divorce Mary. And then, then came the angel.

The angel said, "Joseph, don't be afraid to do what you really want to do. Don't be afraid to risk your reputation. Don't be afraid to take Mary as your wife because God has a part in what is going on here."

The angel was saying, "Joseph, I know about the decision you have made to divorce Mary. I know it must have felt like the right decision at the time, but give it some more thought. Find the courage to change your mind and do that which God is leading you to do." And because of the angel's visit, Joseph changed his mind and the two were married.

Now, that is not to say that Joseph set a precedent for everyone to follow. We all have particular circumstances with which we must deal. However, Joseph does model for us what it is like to struggle with a difficult decision. Joseph handles this decision in a powerful, hopeful way. In Joseph, we find one who is willing to risk being unpopular, one who is willing to reject an easy way out, and one who is willing to face a most difficult circumstance. In Joseph, we find one who takes a courageous stand against the current and then does what is right. When all of his friends surely were urging him to cut his ties and run, Joseph stayed with Mary. It must have been a very lonely decision.

This December eight years ago, over six hundred thousand men and women from the United States found themselves in Saudi Arabia, and Teresa was turning sixteen. Families were torn apart by a military build-up aimed at moving the Iraqis out of Kuwait. Back home and seemingly unaffected by anything going on the world, Teresa had told her mother for over a year what a good sport she could be. She had said that for Christmas and her sixteenth birthday that would follow, she was willing to receive just one gift. Of course, that one gift was what most people want in this society when they turn sixteen — wheels, something to drive. This teenager was rather specific. She wanted a truck, a red and white truck.

So, while parents and spouses and children were learning more about the Middle East than they ever wanted to know, Teresa waited for her sixteenth birthday present. Most every family had a member or a close friend who had either been called to the Persian Gulf or was on stand-by, waiting to be called. People lived in the tension between supporting a nation's troops and holding on to their loved ones. Some questioned the wisdom and motives of Desert Shield and Desert Storm. Others just prayed.

Teresa knew she wasn't going to get a red and white truck, but it was still fun to ask. It had become sort of a game between mother and daughter. "You're still getting me that truck, aren't you, Mom?" "Why, of course, I wouldn't think of getting you anything else." Truck or not, it would be a wonderful Christmas for Teresa and her family, and some playing around and joking with one another only added to the good spirit.

One afternoon Teresa's mother received the perfect item in the mail. Pizza Hut was sending out coupons to people in the area. Attached to the coupons was a magnet to put on the refrigerator. But this was no ordinary magnet. This magnet was in the shape of a truck — a red and white Pizza Hut delivery truck. The mother couldn't wait for her daughter to get home from school to ask one more time about that birthday wish. When Teresa would say, "A red and white truck," the mother planned on fulfilling the daughter's wildest dreams by handing her the magnet in the shape and color of a red and white truck.

School just wasn't as much fun lately. Classmates anxiously awaited news about brothers and sisters and parents who were half a world away. On the bus ride home one boy was confident that his dad would whip the Iraqis' butts, while another child simply stared out the window as if to ask, "Why?"

Teresa's mom watched for the bus from her living room chair. As it drove up, she casually positioned herself around the kitchen table where the daughter regularly ate a snack upon arriving home. Sure enough, the daughter came in and sat down at the table with her mother. Not wanting to give anything away, the mother first asked a couple of questions like, "Did you have a good day? Do you have anywhere to go tonight?"

Then the time was right. Just as the daughter was getting up from the table the mother gently pulled the red and white truck magnet out of her pocket and asked, "Now what did you say you wanted for your birthday and for Christmas?" And without batting an eye the daughter said, "Mother, what I would like most of all is world peace."

The mother sat there stunned in the disappointment of a failed joke. When Teresa had left for school earlier in the day she was a carefree high-schooler who would have been pressed to find Kuwait on a map. Only hours before the mother attempted her joke, Teresa's Christmas spirit focused on what Christmas would bring her in the way of gifts. And then came the angel.

Abraham and Sarah heard the angel, as did Moses and Daniel. An angel spoke to the women at the empty tomb, as well as to the apostles who were in prison, and to Paul in the midst of a storm at sea. But by far, our favorite angel stories are those that have do with this season. An angel promised old Zechariah and barren Elizabeth a son. An angel promised Mary a special baby. An angel directed Joseph to stay with his plans to marry the young woman who was pregnant. And yes, angels even speak to teenagers and moms and people separated from their families and probably all of us at times when we stand fearfully at the crossroads.

Who knows who these angels are? Some people talk about guardian angels in this way, but we are yet to hear of a guardian angel pushing someone to do something difficult or unpopular or risky. From listening to others, it seems guardian angels are more like calming voices that protect people from those sorts of things. Angels in scripture certainly do some of that, but are more often found leading people away from themselves and into the fray. These are angels with messages to do what is right and loving and just. And surely in those difficult times when what is right and loving and just is not clear, the angel comes to calm our fears and direct our thoughts. More and more, these angels sound like the very presence of God.

Most of us can't escape difficult decisions and situations for very long at a time. The decisions range from family matters to financial ones; from health concerns to career choices; from deciding what is right to peer pressure. The decisions we must make are weighty ones involving many factors.

This Christmas we rejoice that we do not make any decision alone. The very promise which the angel brought to Joseph is our promise as well. The angel said, "The virgin shall conceive and bear a son, and they shall name him 'Emmanuel,' which means 'God with us.' " The promise of Emmanuel is that when we are weighing the options carefully in the midst of difficult decisions, we are in the presence of the one true God who is always for us and always with us.

One of these days we will find ourselves telling a friend about the time when we thought we wouldn't make it. The path was too difficult. The decisions were too hard. The journey back was so rough it wasn't worth it. We will tell them about how we trapped ourselves by deciding in favor of self and against God. We will tell them there was no way out.

Our patient friend will look at us and see that we are living, breathing human beings who have meaningful lives and will ask,

"What changed? How were you able to overcome it? Was it really as rough as you say it was for you?"

We will answer, "Yes. It was really that rough. I didn't think I was going to make it ... And then came the angel."

Presents And The Gift Of Presence

Luke 2:1-20

Some of you may have opened gifts before you came here tonight, others may do so later tonight or tomorrow morning. Most of us are to the point that, when you consider gifts from people at school and work and church and clubs, most of December is spent giving to one another. We all agree it is still more blessed to give than to receive, and that would never be in question if the selection of presents was not such a difficult task.

Many men will remember, all too painfully, all the effort given to the selection of gifts for our fathers while they were younger and still living at home. You see, when people live in the same house, one of the greatest temptations to overcome is this tendency to give things to each other that we hope will become community property. "I bet Dad will love this bright yellow tie and I am sure he will wear it often. If not, it does happen to go well with my favorite blue blazer." "I am sure Dad will enjoy this video of pro basketball highlights. He'll probably watch it several nights a week, especially when I am home to watch it with him." Women, who are consistently credited with more sensitivity, probably are guilty of the same kinds of things.

Oh, how patient we are with each other at gift-giving time, and how delightful it is when the tables are turned. The joy comes when the father, who has a closet full of yellow ties and a bookcase loaded with basketball videos, is found perusing the collections of trains in the local toy store. He decides to buy a very expensive train, one with real smoke, a real whistle, and enough track to drive anybody crazy putting it together, but we shouldn't worry. The train is not for him. He says it's for his grandchildren!

John Vannorsdall confessed that for a long time he had taken the short cut with Christmas. He writes, "It became clear, for example, that while I enjoyed receiving well-chosen gifts, I myself was a shopper who invested no time at all in the process. One year I gave everyone staplers. Another year I bought flashlights for everyone, a dozen big, fancy flashlights. It didn't matter whether people needed or wanted one of them, or could afford to replace the six batteries required to operate them.

"I didn't get away with this. People were very nice about the flashlights, pushed all the buttons and said they'd never seen anything like it, but I knew I'd failed. There was a cost to Christmas which wasn't money. It was the cost of thoughtfulness and time, and I knew I had not paid the cost. There are those who prefer Christmas simple. Buy a dozen flashlights. I'm sure Grandma always wanted a flashlight which blinks yellow or red, shines forward and backward, and is too heavy to carry. But thoughtful women and men know that Christmas is much more — considerably more profound and much more satisfying."[1]

The gifts we give, whether they be flashlights and yellow ties or candleholders and coffee mugs, are important symbols which express our love. But they are small tokens compared to the real generosity of this season. Christmas is ultimately about a God whose giving included reaching out through an innocent baby to embrace a hurting world.

In this season one gift transcends all other gifts. A gift which shifts the focus from presents (p-r-e-s-e-n-t-s) to presence (p-r-e-s-e-n-c-e). God's gift of the Christ-child is more significant, of more ultimate value than anything we are able to give. Through the Christ-child, we have life, we know life, and we share life. Because of the Christ-child, we give with a new spirit and a new love and a new freedom. God has shown us the perfect example of giving. Now, we are able to give simply for the love and joy of giving, and our gifts are more than sweaters and ear rings. Now, we can offer a bit of ourselves as a sign that the Christmas spirit has taken root in our lives. Just as God has chosen to be with us, now we can be with others, and for no other reason than to be together.

Henri Nouwen told the story of a student who, many years after graduation, returned to sit in his old professor's office where so many questions had been answered and so many problems had been solved. When the student entered he told his professor that he didn't need anything, he came just to visit, to be together. They sat for a while in silence and looked at each other. One broke the silence by telling the other how nice it was to see each other. The other agreed, and then there was silence. Then the student said, "When I look at you it is as if I am in the presence of Christ." The professor remembers that did not startle or surprise him and that he could only respond with, "It is the Christ in you who recognizes the Christ in me." The student replied with the most healing words Nouwen had heard in many years. "Yes, Christ indeed is in our midst. From now on, wherever you go, or wherever I go, all the ground between us will be holy ground."[2]

Our culture puts such an emphasis on productivity—on doing things, solving problems, making plans, producing products—that two things have happened. In many cases, those who do not solve or plan or produce are looked upon as second class citizens. And secondly, the idea of getting together just for the sake of being together is so foreign that when we do come together we often fail to see the Christ in one another because of this uneasy feeling that we ought to be doing something.

The wonder of this night is that the presence of Christ is with us so that we can genuinely be with each other. No longer must we sit with family members whose divided attention leads to comments like, "She never listens to me." No longer must we sit across from co-workers who half-heartedly hear what we say. No longer must we be at church meetings and plan what we are going to say before the person speaking is ever finished. No longer must we come to worship so unfocused and distracted that we leave unfulfilled.

This is the holiest night of the year. It requires of us reflection and self-examination, and it brings to us the promise that we can be with each other in more meaningful ways. Through the presence of Christ in us, we can recognize the presence of Christ in each other. We can listen and really hear what we are saying to each other. We can share one another's pain and make it our own. We can know of one another's joys and celebrate as if they were our own.

On this night God chooses to be with us so that we might be with one another. May God's love shape our relationships. May God's wisdom guide our decisions. May God's glory touch our ordinary lives. And may God's gift this night live in us and through us, that what we experience in each other is the very presence of Christ.

---

1. John Vannorsdall, "A Touch of Foreboding," *Lectionary Homiletics* (December 1991), pp. 6-7.

2. Henri J. M. Nouwen, *Reaching Out* (New York: Doubleday, 1975), p. 45.

Been There, Done That

Matthew 2:13-23

We can thank Mountain Dew for throwing one more cliché on the heap of cutesy phrases. These popular aphorisms keep their place in the jargon until we wear them out and are forced to trash them. We shouldn't worry though, because by the time that happens there will be three or four more words that we will depend on to explain the totality of human existence.

"Been there, done that" excuses us from having to endure anything a second time. It doesn't matter if we have skateboarded up Mt. Everest, or walked from New York to London, or stood on our heads and gargled peanut butter, we are entirely too cool to do any of that stuff again. "Been there, done that" asks other people not to bore us by requesting that we repeat past experiences. We are too hip for that. Those experiences generated excitement that pumped through our bodies, but please, let's not cover familiar territory. It doesn't matter that some events would be incredible adventures no matter how many times they were experienced. Nor does it matter that something could be learned the second time around that was missed the first time. "Been there, done that" says we aren't going there, or doing that again.

This popular saying means different things to different people. Some places and experiences were so full of disappointment and pain that there isn't much desire to revisit them. We only have to suffer the humiliation of divorce once to know we don't want to do that again. We only have to make ends meet through one stretch of unemployment to know we don't want to go through that again. We only have to hold the hand of one loved through a terminal illness to know that once of that is more than enough. "Been there, done that" not only signals that we don't want to be bored by repeating an old feat, the phrase also declares that there are some things we want to stay as far away from as possible.

As with any cliché, something is lost when we adopt this motto of "Been there, done that." We close doors to exciting possibilities. We fail to see that there is more joy than we have yet known. We miss opportunities to learn from one another. Instead of quickly putting everything behind us with the trite phrase "Been there, done that," perhaps we would be better off recognizing the value of our previous experiences to ourselves and to our sisters and brothers. In a time nearly void of listening skills, in a world which talks a lot about compassion but isn't very compassionate, we need people who remember what it is like to have been there and done that.

Another overused phrase from the 1990s is, "I feel your pain." It gives us some comfort to know that other people feel and share our pain, and we comfort others when we are able to let them know that we hurt with them. People who truly feel our pain are qualified in only one way — they have been there and done that. Before surgery and at the graveside and with the attorney, people tell us, "I know what you are going through." When people say that, they are lying if they have never been prepped for surgery, or if they have never lost somebody that mattered the whole world to them, or if they have never come home to find half of every closet cleaned out.

In the movie *The Doctor,* William Hurt plays the role of a physician who has been diagnosed with cancer. For the first time in his career, he learns firsthand what it is like to be a patient. He discovers the frustration of having to wait forever, the concern of having charts misplaced and tests misread, and the pain and discomfort that come with any number of procedures. As a result, his approach to the practice of medicine changes radically. Because he has been there and done that, the doctor approaches his patients with a new sensitivity. He goes the second mile to ensure that every diagnosis comes only after thorough consideration and that every treatment is handled as humanely and compassionately as possible.[1] It makes a difference when we have been there and done that. Yes, it is true that some people do not learn anything from their past experiences and that some people become bitter and cold from things they have encountered, but there is a blessing to us and to the people around us when we have been there and done that. We approach situations with more insight. We are more patient and credible and understanding toward people in trouble when we remember what it is like to be in trouble ourselves.

Some of the people who speak to our youth about drug abuse ought to be people who have been abusers. They can say things to our children about the temptations and pitfalls that some of us cannot. Some of the people who work with handicapped people should be persons with various physical challenges. They can appreciate the needs of people who are in wheelchairs and on oxygen and confined to their homes better than most of us can.

Some of the counselors who work with divorced people should be people who have known the pain and failure of divorce. They can identify issues for those going through divorce in ways that many people cannot. Some of the people who work with our poor should be people who have survived poverty themselves. They can offer encouragement and compassion that those of us who have only known one good break after another cannot.

And when Matthew told the story of Jesus' birth and his early years, Matthew thought that it was important for Jesus to have been there and done that. Jesus impresses people for different reasons. Some love the miracle stories. Others are drawn to his teaching. Still others are moved by his interaction with the unlovely and unlovable. In this lesson, another attraction to Jesus surfaces.

This lesson calls for Joseph, Mary, and Jesus to begin the first leg of a long and winding journey. Yet another angel appears to Joseph in a dream and the family is on their way to Egypt, and we don't even want to know why. We don't want to hear anything about another holiday season disaster, but we know the story. King Herod is about to search for this child named Jesus. In a ridiculous mismatch, the King is out to destroy a baby. Out of a concern for safety, Joseph heads out in the middle of the night and carries Mary and their newborn to Egypt. They will stay there until the word comes that Herod has died.

All too early we find Jesus on the move, with every new place presenting fresh and demanding challenges. Instead of keeping office hours, Jesus moved around. Some encounters brought trick questions by those trying to destroy his reputation. Some experiences were with the outcasts who were shunned by the respectable people of the day. Some exchanges were shocking. Every street corner and every bend in the road found Jesus going here and there — up to the mountains to pray, alongside the shore to teach, to the bedside of a friend's mother to heal, and to a second-floor room for one last meal together.

All of these journeys of Jesus start in this passage in which he moves from Bethlehem to Egypt to Judea before settling in Nazareth. It is no coincidence that this journey included a stop in Egypt. The central event in the Jewish faith is the exodus from slavery in Egypt. Over and over again the people were told, "Remember that you were a slave in the land of Egypt, and the Lord your God redeemed you" (Deuteronomy 15:15). Even if it was a brief sojourn as a child, or even if it was symbolic, Matthew wanted to show that Jesus knew what life had been like for God's people.

More than that, this trip through Egypt is a sign of what life will be like for Jesus. Jesus will know pain firsthand and will suffer interminably. While some are mesmerized by the divine side of Jesus, it is his human side which allows us to relate to him and which promises that he relates to us. Like all of us, Jesus wept, suffered disappointment, and experienced betrayal. Like all of us, Jesus was hungry and thirsty and lonely and tempted. If Jesus is a friend who knows all our sorrows, it is because our sorrows are so very much like his own.

"Out of Egypt I have called my son." Jesus' emergence from the place where his people once were treated brutally as slaves serves to call us out of our own places and times of suffering with the assurance that we are never alone. The spirit of the one who knew of the suffering in Egypt and knew suffering in his own life is with us. Out of Egypt, out of pain and suffering, out of mistrust and hostility, we are called. Of course, the only way out of Egypt, the only way out of the despair that grips us, is through the pain, not around it. There are no shortcuts. There is no denying the hurt, but neither is there denying the one who leads us out of Egypt and promises that bit by bit we will find more life than we are experiencing at the present.

Out of Egypt we are called. We are called to come through the pain that has visited us. We are called to get our own faith on the move. We are called to re-engage life in its most abundant form. And we are called to make a credible and exciting witness to those still stuck in Egypt. For while we may have been set free from the pain that was gripping us, others continue to suffer. They are overwhelmed by life's disappointments, drained by life's losses, and crushed by life's blows.

Lest we forget and become arrogant and insensitive and apathetic, our call for this and every season is to be with the hurting among us, even as God is with us through the presence of Jesus. We can say some things to them out of our experiences that they desperately need to hear. We embody hope and promise for those who are hurting because we have endured and survived our troubles. As real as their pain is, we are able to reassure them that there is more to their lives than the pain that presently threatens to destroy them.

After trying everything else, Shelly was present for her first Alcoholics Anonymous meeting. Skeptical and listening half-heartedly at first, the words of Martha caught her attention. Martha told the group, "I just knew that I could handle alcohol and my other problems on my own, but I couldn't. Seven years ago I came to my first A.A. meeting and since that time I have grown as a person beyond anything I could have ever imagined."

Martha exuded confidence and depth. She spoke of her higher power, the God of Jesus Christ, and the way in which God now lived at the center of her life. Her words oozed with sincere encouragement and concern. Most of all, Martha exhibited a thankfulness which words could not express. Shelly, who came to the meeting doubtful that anything she would hear would change the way she felt or thought, made her way to Martha when the meeting was over. "I want what you have," Shelly told Martha, "I want what you have."

Shelly wanted the compassion and depth and hope which Martha knew, but she may not have realized fully how Martha came to know those things. Martha learned compassion from a time of deep personal suffering. She acquired spiritual depth from hours of praying when there was nowhere else to turn. She discovered hope by taking one step at a time because "one day at a time" was too much to be expected.

Shelly said, "I want what you have. Where do I get it?" And Martha told her, "It comes from being right where you are and doing just what you are doing." Martha went on to tell Shelly the oddest story about learning compassion when we are hurting, and learning love when we are excluded, and learning hope when we are helpless. Martha knew. She had been there and done that.

---

1. *The Doctor*, Touchstone Home Videos.

In The Flesh

John 1:(1-9) 10-18

"And the Word became flesh."

We hear those words so easily that they are lost on us. We quickly associate them with the baby in Bethlehem's manger, and rightly so, but then we dismiss them without being startled or shocked or even mildly surprised. "The Word became flesh," the gospel writer says, and we yawn in agreement.

Some of the Greeks didn't yawn. They were appalled at such a thought and quickly acted to correct what they thought of as a ludicrous, even sacrilegious thought. It wasn't that God could not have become flesh, but why would God have wanted to become flesh? By their way of thinking, the flesh was bad and the body was evil. If they could have found some way to live outside the body they would have, but they couldn't come up with anything. So, they tolerated the body as a necessary way to "house the soul."

We aren't ready to give up on the Greeks altogether. We too slip into this mind set that the soul is good and spiritual, and the body is bad and carnal. In April of 1996 Baylor University, a Baptist school in Texas, did the unthinkable. The school not only allowed, but sanctioned a campus-wide dance. There are more jokes about Baptists not being allowed to dance than there are Baptists, and that's why this is major news. Most Baptists traditionally have frowned on dancing because of the slippery-slope argument that dancing surely will lead to other things that are even worse than dancing. At the root of this is the idea that physical expression is bad and should take a back seat to the higher and purer gifts of the mind and the soul.

The Greek word behind flesh in this lesson is the same word Paul uses over and over to describe human nature in all its weakness and sin.[1] In other words, when God became flesh God immediately became acquainted with all the desires, problems, and temptations inherent in human life, which is one more reason why the Word becoming flesh isn't all that desirable. Who wants a God who is so much like us? We want a God who rules over the earth, who gives power and dominion to human beings, and whose knowledge and goodness are always beyond reproach.

But isn't that the point of John's statement? There is in the earth the presence of the Holy One. The Eternal has appeared in time. The God whom no one has seen has become visible. The inaccessible One is now available to us. The Word became flesh is not a sign that the great God has been diminished to the lesser stature of humanity, but that the great God has paid us a visit in human form.

It's not the first time God's presence was made known, and it won't be the last. God is always looking for a place to dwell. God is present in the words of scripture, in the beauty of a painting, in majestic architecture, and in the stirring drama of great literature. God was present at the Red Sea, and at Mount Sinai, and in the foreign land where the people were held in captivity. But God did not become a book, or a painting, or a building. God took on human form. The Word became flesh.

A popular song asks, "If God had a face, what would it look like?" Maybe the question should be rephrased as a statement. "God has a face, and it looks like your face, and my face, and the faces of humans everywhere." If people want to know what God looks like, and they do, they are going to look at us. People who will come to experience something of God's presence will not arrive at that moment by persuasive arguments or logical thinking or scientific proof. More than likely, they will come to know what God is like through knowing God's people. People who experience love do not do so by reading about it in a book. They experience love through other human beings. There is much for people to read about God in scripture and elsewhere, but not much of it will hold water unless they come to know women and men, youth and children, who appear in the flesh in the same way that God appears on the page.

That doesn't mean we have to be perfect people, but it does call us to take seriously the fact that our bodies are God's temple and God's spirit dwells in our flesh (1 Corinthians 3:16). We can't be perfect people, but we can be so responsive to the spirit of God that "the life of Jesus may be made visible in our mortal flesh" (2 Corinthians 4:11). It means that we not only see the heart or soul as religious, but that we love the Lord our God with all our heart, soul, mind and strength" (Mark 12:30) and that we present our "bodies as a living sacrifice, holy and acceptable to God, which is our spiritual worship" (Romans 12:1-2). Our existence is not about worshiping God with our souls and treating our bodies as if they were our own. Our earthly life is not about having a pure heart and paying no attention to our physical needs. Instead, we are about presenting our whole selves in faithful stewardship to God because we carry the good news in these bodies of ours, as well as in our hearts and minds.

In the 1995 General Assembly of the Christian Church (Disciples of Christ), the church adopted a mission statement which calls the church "to be and to share the good news of Jesus Christ." We cannot share the good news until we become the good news. We are to become the good news in the flesh for the world to see.

It's always nice to hear people say, "Oh, I drove through your town last week and saw your church. It's beautiful." They are right, of course, but they only saw a part of the church. They only saw the building. They missed the best part. If they only drove through they didn't have time to see all those occasions when the church becomes the good news, when the Word becomes flesh. And the Word becomes flesh all over the place.

People volunteer time and money to prepare and deliver meals to those confined to their homes, and the Word becomes flesh. Church members visit those who have lost loved ones, and the Word becomes flesh. Mission teams respond to disasters that destroyed the towns of people they have never met, and the Word becomes flesh. A young man gives up a year's salary to fund scholarships for children who lost their parents in the Oklahoma City bombing, and the Word becomes flesh. Parents travel to Romania to adopt sick orphans, and the Word becomes flesh. A woman calls her neighbor every morning to make sure she is okay, and the Word becomes flesh. Friends wait with a husband at the hospital while his wife is having surgery, and the Word becomes flesh. The minister takes communion to those who cannot attend worship, and the Word becomes flesh.

And anyone who has ever delivered meals or visited the bereaved or responded to a disaster or given sacrificially or taken people in or sat with friends in a difficult time knows that what we give pales in comparison to what we get back. It's not just that the Word becomes flesh in our actions, but that the Word is already flesh in those to whom we minister. The courage of a woman who lives alone speaks to us, and the Word becomes flesh. The faith of a family waiting for the surgeon to come out makes a powerful witness, and the Word becomes flesh. The people who are rebuilding after the storm embody a hope that we desperately needed to see, and the Word becomes flesh. When we see that the foster or adoptive family is learning and receiving as much from the child as the child is from them we are reminded of all the people in our lives from whom we could learn more of the truth, and the Word becomes flesh.

The decline that so many churches are experiencing is baffling since we live in a time when there is a desperate need for community. People are less and less concerned about what church name a congregation has, and more and more concerned with finding a supportive, receptive, loving congregation that will welcome and take care of them. There is a lot of debate about various issues, but people who are hurting aren't looking for position statements. They are looking for the Word that gives life and comfort and hope, and they are looking right at us to see if that Word has any flesh on it.

The Word becoming flesh is a powerful statement about God's presence in Jesus, but it is also more. The Word becoming flesh leads us toward one another, pointing us toward a new community where we see the truth and dignity in all of God's children. The Word becoming flesh reminds us that the truth and light live in us. Yet, we know none of us are capable of holding all the truth and light, so we need and depend on each other for pieces of the truth and light that we do not yet have.

If we are all made in the image of God, if we are all distinct revelations of God, then we all carry within us some message and experience that the rest of us need to hear. Christine Smith writes about how we further insult the marginalized people by not listening to the truth they embody. Smith says that people who are older, handicapped, of a different class or race or sexual orientation all embody some word which deserves our attention. That is, they carry in the flesh some image of their Creator, some truth which would lead us to deeper understanding, and some gifts which would enhance our world.[2]

May we become and then share the good news. More than that, may we be open to the good news which all the people of the earth embody, learning and receiving from them as much as they learn and receive from us. May the love of God which we talk about so freely be recognized in the love of human beings like us.

Jerry had lived down the street from the church for nine years, but no one in the church or the neighborhood knew him very well. He didn't participate in the church or community. One afternoon his wife suffered a major stroke, and all there was to do was wait. Jerry and his three children waited 39 days in the hospital, but they didn't wait alone. Every single day of that 39-day stretch somebody from the church stopped by to say hello. Two church members drove grandchildren back and forth to school, ball games, and dances. Another church member mowed Jerry's yard and watered his flowers. Another person from the church transferred sick days from her account to Jerry's account so that Jerry would continue to receive a salary. During that time the people from the church got to know Jerry and came to appreciate him very much. On the day when Jerry's wife died, people from church were there.

And the Word became flesh.

---

1. William Barclay, *The Gospel of John,* Volume 1 (Philadelphia: Westminster Press, 1975), p. 65.

2. Christine Smith, *Preaching as Weeping, Confession, and Resistance: Radical Responses to Radical Evil* (Louisville: Westminster/John Knox Press, 1992).

Going Ahead Anyway

Matthew 2:1-12

Did you notice that bad things did not stop happening through the holidays? And is any warning necessary that bad things will happen in every season of this year? Surely there is better news than that, but we ought to be honest about the bad news. Not even the holidays generate enough good will to stop people from blowing up airplanes and destroying people's reputations and abusing children and selling drugs to teenagers and gunning down their neighbors.

In fact, the holidays often elevate stress levels. People spend money they don't have on gifts, and the financial strain creates worry. People miss loved ones so much that the joy is hollow. Others find the stress of their families being together to be so great that they dread the holiday reunions. For these and other reasons, the times that are supposed to be the most joyous are often filled with tension and anxiety. While there is much good to celebrate, it shouldn't surprise us that some of humanity's worst moments are on display during this time.

The persistent presence of evil causes us to long for this Sunday, or any Sunday, in which the presence of God in the world is recognized and celebrated. A quick glance at the newspaper headlines or an efficient surf of the cable stations presents enough bad news. We are in need of good news, and it needs to be good news that is at least equal to the bad news. Those who are struggling need to know that they do not struggle alone. Those who are grieving need to know that they do not grieve alone. All of us, regardless of what circumstances or challenges we face, need to know that there is strength and hope that will outlast the evil of the day.

So what response do we make to the evil around us? One response is to explain the evil. From the beginning of time, people have sought to explain the presence of evil in our world. If we can understand the source of evil and how it wrecks our lives, maybe we can figure out a way to stop it. One of the themes in the story of Job is that of trying to explain the bad things that had happened to him. When Job lost his property, his children, and his health, friends arrived to explain why these horrible things had happened. Eliphaz, Bildad, and Zophar persistently tried to convince Job that he must have done something wrong. Otherwise, why would he be suffering?

There are people who try to explain the evil to us. A tornado rips through our town and some neighbor with good intentions says, "It must have happened for a reason." Of course, there is never a good reason for something like that to happen. Some good things may come from it, but there's no good reason beforehand for a tornado to destroy lives and property and dreams.

Jerry Falwell has said that AIDS is God's punishment on this country for frequent abortions and widespread homosexuality. It eases people's fears when we can explain AIDS in that manner, but it also raises a lot of questions. Is that the way God relates to us? And if so, what sins have we committed to account for all the other illnesses and diseases that plague us?

A blanket explanation used to explain everything from a toothache to an earthquake is "the will of God." No matter how horrible the event may have been, some are content to say that it must have been the will of God. For some reason, people find comfort in their losses if they can explain the car wreck and the heart attack and the factory closing as being the will of God. Who knows, maybe those things are the will of God, but if they are then we are left to explain why a loving God wills for those bad things to happen.

A number of people mistakenly refer to Harold Kushner's best-selling book as *Why Bad Things Happen to Good People*. That's the question everybody wants answered, but that is not the title of Kushner's book. Nor is that the point of his book. The correct title of the book is *When Bad Things Happen to Good People*. Isn't that the best we can do? We can spend years wondering why, but it is beyond human capacity to make sense of most tragedies. We can try our best to explain evil, but most of it is beyond explanation.

Another way to deal with evil is to eliminate it altogether. It sounds impossible, but there are folks working around the clock trying to rid our communities and world of evil. Various levels of government constantly are providing resources and services to ease human suffering. Vaccines are given to young children to guard against crippling and even fatal diseases. Nutritional supplements are made available to people of different ages and backgrounds to help maintain good health. Federal officials negotiate with other countries with the hope that war and unnecessary devastation might be prevented.

People are working in other ways to eliminate evil in all its manifestations. Tremendous amounts of money are devoted to research with the hope that cures to our most dreaded diseases will be found. All sorts of technological developments may point the way to a better quality of life for us all. Educational programs are geared to equip us with the knowledge necessary to deal with everything from crime in our communities to adopting a healthier diet. Progress is being made in encouraging and producing better citizenship. A lot of evil is eliminated when people resolve their conflicts in a civil way. Every time anger is channeled in a positive way, evil is curbed. Every time groups handle their differences of opinion in a mature way, possible acts of evil are averted.

Evil not only comes when the hurricane trashes a town or the x-ray reveals bad news. We recognize evil in the abusive parent and the manipulative friend and the irresponsible spouse. Despite our best efforts, we are not going to eliminate all the evil around us, or even within us. We don't always agree on how we should tackle certain problems. Some people continue to benefit from the evil in the world and they are not likely to work to turn things around. Evil persists in such a magnitude that eliminating it seems very unlikely. The problems are numerous, the suffering is great, and the sources are so uncontrollable that we will never eliminate evil.

So, we can't explain evil and we can't eliminate it. What now? The only answer that we have for this problem of evil is to work around it. It's the only solution we have ever had. Evil is here to stay. However, that does not mean it is time to give up or give in. Instead, it is time to recommit ourselves to what is right and good and compassionate, and to work in whatever ways we can to minimize the impact of evil in our lives and communities and world.

That is what people did with King Herod, who seemed to have more evil in him than most people. Jesus would never have seen his second birthday if Herod's plan had worked. Herod first became frightened when he heard that a lot of people were paying tribute to Jesus. Then Herod learned when and where Jesus was born. He thought he had some wise men tricked into returning to him with the information about where Jesus could be found, but the wise men were forewarned and they did not return to the king.

We know the rest of the story. After Herod realized he had been outwitted, he ordered for all the children around Bethlehem to be killed who were two years old and under. Of course, that's when Joseph, Mary, and Jesus took off to Egypt. They returned only after they heard the news of Herod's death. A large part of the anxiety was created by the fact that Herod was such an evil person. Herod destroyed practically everybody who was any threat to his power, including adherents of religious groups. He executed 45 Sadducees and confiscated their property. Herod conspired to have one person drowned, and later executed his wife, mother-in-law, and brother-in-law.[1]

In short, Herod was a power-hungry ruler whose actions reeked of evil. We can't explain his actions, or the actions of anybody else who acts in evil ways. And despite our best efforts to create an atmosphere of cooperation and kindness, it is unrealistic to think we are going to eliminate from the face of the earth divisive, rude, evil people. Our only choice, unless we want to give in or give up, is to work around the evil. Yes, this is an imperfect world, but that does not relieve us of our responsibility to work for what is good and right. If anything, the evil present in our world only accentuates the need for us to do something.

Someone penned a few thoughts and titled the piece "Anyway."[2]

People are unreasonable, illogical, and self-centered.
   Love them anyway!
If you do good, people will accuse you of selfish, ulterior motives.
   Do good anyway!
If you are successful, you will win false friends and true enemies.
   Succeed anyway!
The good you do today will be forgotten tomorrow.
   Do good anyway!
Honesty and frankness will make you vulnerable.
   Be honest and frank anyway!
The biggest people with the biggest ideas can be shot down by the smallest people with the smallest minds.
   Think big anyway!
People favor underdogs but follow only top dogs.
   Fight for some underdogs anyway!
What you spend years building may be destroyed overnight.
   Build anyway!
People really need help but may attack you if you help them.
   Help people anyway!
Give the world the best you have and you will get kicked in the teeth.
   Give the world the best you have anyway!

There are always going to be poor people around, but that didn't stop Mother Teresa from doing more than her part to help those she could. Many people in our country are kept out of owning a home for various reasons, but that hasn't kept Jimmy Carter from driving nails and painting walls for Habitat for Humanity. There may never be widespread peace in the Middle East, but that hasn't stopped any number of people from devoting their time and talents toward creating pockets and places of peace. College and professional sports are riddled with cheaters, but that hasn't kept some people from playing by the rules.

People responsible for things like Pan Am Flight 103 and the Oklahoma City bombing will continue to live in this world, as will people who destroy their families and create unnecessary conflict at work, but we must not let them have the final word. Churches will always have people who create problems, but we are not going to quit supporting the work of the church. On lots of days we will feel like we are not appreciated for what we do, but that doesn't mean we are going to stop doing what we do. We are going to be treated badly from time to time, but we are going to keep believing that love will win out. People will abuse the welfare system, but that doesn't mean we are going to turn our backs on those we are called to serve. Diseases are going to continue to strike, but we are going to continue to support the research that will one day cure those diseases.

A lot of these situations test our commitment. It's easy to love the church when things are going well. Anybody can cheer for a winning basketball team. We are attracted to problems that have easy solutions. However, how committed we are in the face of monumental challenges reveals how deeply we believe in something. When problems arise and conflict erupts and support erodes, we are forced to make a decision. Will we let the presence of evil in all its many forms cause us to back down or step back or give up, or will we recognize the problems but go ahead anyway?

It's not a hypothetical situation. It's the reality in which we live. It's the question before us, right now. And a hungry, hurting world awaits our response.

---

1. Bruce M. Metzger and Michael D. Coogan, eds., *The Oxford Companion to the Bible* (New York: Oxford University Press, 1993), pp. 281-82.

2. Source unknown.

Baptism In Three Movements

Matthew 3:13-17

There are two very different ways to think about baptism. The first approach recognizes the time of baptism as a saving moment in which the person being baptized accepts the love and forgiveness of God. The person then considers herself "saved." She may grow in the faith through the years, but nothing which she will experience after her baptism will be as important as her baptism. She always will be able to recall her baptism as the time when her life changed.

The second approach wouldn't disagree with any of that, but would add to it significantly. This idea affirms baptism as the time when God's love and forgiveness are experienced. It also recognizes baptism as a time of change. However, where the first approach isolates the act of baptism as the most important moment, the second approach understands baptism more as a beginning. While it is true that in the waters of baptism God laid claim on our lives, it is also true that we spend the rest of our lives trying to figure out what that means. The first understanding often overlooks the journey which follows baptism.

Baptism too frequently carries the connotation of having arrived. Sometimes people say to their ministers, "I want to be baptized and join the church as soon as I get my life in order." Of course, if that is what any of us are waiting on, we will never be baptized. None of us will ever have our lives sufficiently in order to be baptized. Baptism is not something we earn, nor is it a sign that we have found all the answers. Nothing could be further from the truth.

Baptism is a beginning. It is the desire to see the world differently, to see each other differently, and even to see ourselves differently. Baptism is a fresh start, not a destination. Baptism calls into question our previous lives, it does not bless them. Baptism is not a trial-free membership, but a rite of initiation into a way of life in which Jesus promised there would be trials.

Jesus' baptism serves as a model for our baptism. For Jesus, baptism represents the beginning of his ministry. While some ultimate questions may have been answered when he was with John the Baptist in the Jordan River, Jesus continued to deal with questions and temptations throughout his life. The baptism of Jesus is one of our favorite stories. We love to hear how the heavens opened, to imagine the dove descending, and to hear God's blessing on the Son. We would like to think something like that happens when we are baptized. What we should be prepared for is that our journey of faith, much like Jesus' journey, continues to unfold long after our baptism as we try to discern what our baptism means in our daily living.

We can begin to understand more about our baptism by thinking of it in three ways.[1] First, baptism is about beginning anew. It is a fresh start, even when we are fairly comfortable and satisfied with our old lives. Paul said we emerge from baptism to walk "in newness of life" (Romans 6:4). There are two ways to make something new. We can start with nothing and make something new, or we can start with what we already have and make that new. Baptism transforms our lives and we think, speak, live, and act in ways that represent to the world the image of Christ.

Baptism transforms stinginess into generosity, narrow-mindedness into thoughtful consideration, and prejudice into love. Baptism transforms our fear of one another into a desire for true community, our suspicious motives into open, honest dialogue, and our hesitancy into boldness. Baptism transforms groups of people into churches, gatherings of individuals into a family of brothers and sisters, and church services into times of worship.

Does all that happen when we are baptized? No, but those are the kinds of things that happen through our lives as we continue to be open to what our baptism means to us. The Christian life at its best is an ongoing transformation in which we continue to be shaped by the presence of Christ within us.

In Ephesians 4, which discusses many of the implications of baptism, we are shown what this new life looks like. We are urged to lead a life worthy of our calling, and then we are told that such a life entails humility, gentleness, and patience. We are to bear with one another in love, and are to make every effort to maintain unity in the body. The church in general has a reputation of rising to the great occasions — the special celebration, the response to the hurricane, our concern for the dying — but forgetting in between those times what life in the Spirit involves. Humility, gentleness, and patience won't get much coverage on the evening news, but those are marks of the Christian life.

Yet, who among us has mastered those things in our relationships with our sisters and brothers? We know the kind of trouble that is caused by thinking of ourselves too highly and not regarding others with the kind of appreciation they are due, but true humility is not something very many people spend their days trying to achieve. We know the problems created by bulldozing our way through every meeting and every conversation, but it seems to get our point across and our agenda passed more effectively than being gentle. We know that some things simply are not going to happen on our schedule and that some things may never happen, but being patient seems too much like not doing anything. In short, humility, gentleness, and patience are sometimes in short supply, but not so among those who are engaged in this lifelong process of growth. We are continually about the business of deepening our spiritual lives by being transformed by the newness which Christ's presence in our lives guarantees.

The second part of baptism is the good news that we have been included. You may remember the episode of *The Andy Griffith Show* in which the Women's Historical Society had discovered that a living descendant of a Revolutionary War hero was living right there in Mayberry. The news generated excitement and curiosity throughout the town as people made plans for recognizing the hero's relative. Barney Fife, of course, twisted his own family tree to the point that he put himself in line for the honor. The rest of the towns-people felt special just because someone among them was related to the hero.

Everyone was shocked when the news came. A careful analysis of the genealogical records determined that the hero's descendant was Otis Campbell, the town drunk. Despite instructions to find a "substitute Otis" for the presentation, the real Otis showed up for the ceremony. When the ladies gave him the plaque which they had engraved especially for him, Otis gave the plaque to the town. He said, "Just because you're the descendant of a hero doesn't make you one. So I would like to present this plaque to the town of Mayberry, to which I am just proud to belong."

Well, aren't we all? Aren't we all just happy to belong, to be included! We can refer to this part of our baptism as incorporation. We are included, incorporated into the body of Jesus Christ. This incorporation came about as a result of a love that was determined to draw us in. And long after the act of baptism, that love holds us together without ranking us as more or less important, allows us to disagree with each other without deserting one another, and leads us to use our different gifts without any need to compare them with somebody else's gifts.

Our baptism is personal, but it is not private. We are included alongside others. The waters of baptism are not only symbolic of being cleansed from sin, but also of the power baptism has to break down barriers between people. We share a common relationship with Jesus Christ in which the old divisions and designations no longer apply. While this part of baptism can be called incorporation, it is easy to see how transformation is necessary in order for us to live with all who have been included by God's love. Baptism is not about being incorporated into the body with no intention of living and working with the other members of the body. As we are included alongside others, we realize that for the body to be healthy all must be transformed. As we are transformed, we are more likely to expand the circle of our love to include others as full partners in the church.

The third part of baptism is ordination. With baptism comes the Spirit, and with the Spirit come gifts to be used in the service of

God. When Lindsey Davis was elected bishop in the United Methodist Church, he reminded all of us of the basis for ministry. "It isn't ordination or consecration, but baptism that makes us servants of Christ and the church."[2] We too often view ministry as that which the minister does, but ministry is the work in which all baptized believers engage in response to the call and claim of God on our lives.

Baptism was ordination for Jesus. It was the beginning of his ministry. In our time we ordain ministers, and sometimes elders and deacons, but we have removed from our understanding of baptism the conviction that our lives are to be offered in service. When we enter the household of God, we do so with a vocation, the belief that God has called us to some particular work that will utilize our gifts in building up the body and in making a better world.

To understand baptism as an ordination for all Christians is not a ploy on the part of ministers to get church members to do more work. In fact, the area in which your gifts may be the most useful may not even be in the church. You may find your gift to be teaching a young child to read. Another person's gift may be in organizing a community protest against the proposed chemical factory that wants to move into town. Another person's gift may be helping the working homeless to find a decent, safe place to live. Baptism comes with a vocation, and it is not a burden. When seen through the lens of baptism, our work is a joyful response to the love we have experienced.

Garrison Keillor tells the story of Larry the Sad Boy. Larry the Sad Boy was saved twelve times, which is an all-time record in the Lutheran Church. In the Lutheran Church there is no altar call, no organist playing "Just As I Am," and no minister with shiny hair manipulating the congregation. These are Lutherans, and they repent the same way that they sin — discreetly and tastefully. Keillor writes, "Granted, we're born in original sin and are worthless and vile, but twelve conversions is too many. God didn't mean us to feel guilty all our lives. There comes a point when you should dry your tears and join the building committee and start grappling with the problems of the church furnace and the church roof and make church coffee and be of use."[3]

A part of baptism is ordination, a call to serve. When we serve, we will encounter others who have been incorporated into the body and we will be challenged to see how our gifts complement the gifts of others. Also, as we work side by side, we will find that our humility, gentleness, and patience may be tested from time to time. In those moments we will realize that our transformation is still in process and we must not give up on it. In all of these things, baptism is a beginning.

The story is told of a pastor's words to a baby shortly after he had baptized her. No doubt, the minister was speaking as much to the congregation as to the infant. "Little sister, by this act of baptism, we welcome you to a journey that will take your whole life. This isn't the end. It's the beginning of God's experiment with your life. What God will make of you, we know not. Where God will take you, surprise you, we cannot say. This we do know and this we say — God is with you."[4]

And God will be with us as we live out our baptism.

———————

1. Malcolm Warford, Lecture at Lexington Theological Seminary, Lexington, Kentucky, May, 1996.

2. Lindsey Davis, quoted in *The Bulletin*, Lexington Theological Seminary, August, 1996.

3. Garrison Keillor, "The Exiles," *Listening for God*, Paula J. Carlson and Peter S. Hawkins, eds. (Minneapolis: Augsburg Press, 1994), p. 120.

4. William H. Willimon and Stanley Hauerwas, *Resident Aliens* (Nashville: Abingdon Press, 1989), pp. 52-53.

1/14/07

You May Have
To Die First

John 1:29-42

"**Well,** I don't know what will happen now. We've got some
difficult days ahead. But it doesn't matter with me now. Because
I've been to the mountaintop. And I don't mind. Like anybody, I
would like to live a long life. Longevity has its place. But I'm not
concerned about that now. I just want to do God's will. And he's
allowed me to go up to the mountain. And I've looked over. And
I've seen the promised land. I may not get there with you. But I
want you to know tonight, that we, as a people will get to the promised land. And I'm happy, tonight. I'm not worried about anything.
I'm not fearing any [man]. Mine eyes have seen the glory of the
coming of the Lord."[1]

Those words, spoken by Martin Luther King, Jr., the night before he was assassinated in Memphis, still haunt us. To this day,
they generate speculation and debate. Some are convinced that King
knew he would be killed. With the kind of turmoil King was creating and the general upheaval that was being witnessed from court-
house squares to college campuses, it doesn't require much imagination to envision a scenario wherein King would be gunned down.
King noted on that very night that the "... nation is sick. Trouble is
in the land. Confusion all around."[2] Others are equally certain that
King did not have a premonition about his own death. John
Cartwright, who holds the professorship at Boston University which
bears King's name, believes that King was not predicting his own
death. Rather, according to Cartwright, Dr. King was only aware
that the arc of justice is long and that significant changes only happen over an extended period of time. In other words, King knew

that his words might articulate the dream, but the reality of the dream might not be experienced until generations later.[3]

We have debated the same issue with Jesus. Did Jesus know he was going to die? Did God send Jesus to earth to die? Or, as events evolved and pressure mounted, did it then become evident to Jesus that his faithfulness to God may bring about his own death? There are those who believe that Bethlehem and Calvary were interwoven into Jesus' life from the beginning. When John the Baptist declared that Jesus was the Lamb of God, it sounded like Jesus' crucifixion was certain from the outset. In a culture that sacrificed lambs twice a day in the temple, those words are a kiss of death. "Here is the Lamb of God" can be loosely understood to mean, "Hey, look here, everyone, here's the one that is going to be sacrificed." This Lamb of God imagery says something very different from "light of the world" or "bread of life" imagery. Jesus as the light of the world illumines and brings warmth. Jesus as the bread of life satisfies our deepest spiritual and physical hunger. Jesus as the Lamb of God speaks of one who was on his way to the cross.

Leslie Weatherhead disagreed with those who believe Jesus was destined to die on the cross from the beginning, saying that God's plan was for people to follow Jesus, not kill him.[4] The purpose of Jesus, from this point of view, was for Jesus to reveal the love of God, teach about God's ways, and proclaim God's rule in the world. The problem with assuming that Jesus was sent to die is that we don't take seriously the subversive nature of Jesus' ministry. Jesus railed against established practices and comfortable people. In the end, Jesus was killed by religious and political leaders who were threatened by his presence. We tend to forget or ignore those parts of the story which show Jesus in trouble. We are more attracted to the feeding of the five thousand than we are to the hometown folks who tried to stone Jesus after he preached a sermon. We are more fond of the woman who pressed through the crowd to touch the hem of Jesus' garment than we are of those who told Jesus to go away.

The arc of justice is long, indeed. Some problems don't seem any closer to being solved now than they ever were. Even when the changes are for the good, there is resistance and opposition from those who are making a huge profit from things being the way they are now. Do you remember that story Luke tells of Jesus healing a demon-possessed man (Luke 8:26-39)? The demons left the man and went into a herd of pigs who proceeded to run over a cliff. Apparently the townspeople were more concerned about who was going to pay for the pigs than they were about the man who had been delivered from his illness. After all, they didn't thank Jesus or have a parade for him. They ran him out of town! Things were changing and people were becoming very frightened. The solution was to get rid of the person behind the changes.

The same thing happened to Paul and Silas. A woman was possessed by some kind of spirit that supposedly gave her psychic powers. Paul and Silas were preaching in the area and this woman became a nuisance. Paul turned to the woman and ordered the spirit to come out of her, and it did! Now, wasn't that good news? No, their actions landed Paul and Silas in jail and nearly got them killed. The people who were making money of this fortune-teller didn't appreciate Paul's healing powers very much (Acts 16:16-24).

We see it everyday. Somebody tries to change the way state government contracts are awarded and before the sun goes down the person has been run out of the capital by those who benefit from the way contracts presently are awarded. We may not be able to find a telephone number to call if we have a problem with a health insurance claim, but when a proposal is on the table to re-vamp the healthcare system we can bet the insurance companies will be calling us for our support. Everyone wants more facilities to treat troubled children, but when one comes to our neighborhood and threatens to lower our property taxes, we may not favor the facility as much as we once thought we did. It is hard to stomach the fact that not everybody wants people healed and families strengthened and communities restored. Not everybody wants racial harmony and economic equality and matching opportunities.

Some difference is made by our efforts. A foster family welcomes a troubled child into their home and one less child is left to survive our violent streets. A church does ministry with Hispanic migrant workers and at least some strangers are welcomed and loved. A youth group takes part of its summer vacation to rebuild homes and playgrounds among Appalachia's poor. Christians of all races work together to stop the burning of black churches. Men and women gather weekly in Bible study to discern the mind of Christ and to appropriate it for their own lives. Some of our efforts bear fruit. Some positive changes occur. We may never see other changes. The arc of justice, after all, is long, and we are left to decide how important these causes are. Are they important enough for us to give our efforts to them even though we may never benefit from them or see their completion?

We should realize that sometimes in the course of this long arc of justice there is death. Some black preacher from the South, equipped with an advanced degree from one of the North's premier schools, begins preaching and everybody is okay with that. Then the preacher's words lead to bold actions on the part of the people. Established boundaries are challenged. Traditional ways of doing things are questioned. Demands are made. Changes are planned. People don't like what's happening. Maybe they all didn't want Dr. King dead, but those who didn't still wanted to construct obstacles enough to suppress the dream and silence the dreamer.

One minister surrounded himself at the church chancel with children during worship and began to talk to them about the upcoming holiday. When asked whose birthday would be celebrated, the well-informed group responded, "Martin Luther King, Jr." The minister inquired further by asking what kind of work King did. How much prompting it took is not certain, but the answer being fished for was given. "Martin Luther King, Jr., was the minister of a church."

In an attempt to draw an obvious parallel, the minister reminded the gathered faithful that was also his life's work. At that point, with a straightening of the necktie and some posturing which made him look a bit taller and a lot more distinguished, the minister wondered aloud about the possibility of a holiday being named for him. Across a couple of rows of pews came an innocent whisper that must have sounded like Jesus himself: "You have to die first."[5]

Who knows whether Jesus thought he would die for what he said and did, but either way it didn't seem to get in the way of his faithfulness. There is a price to pay for a faithfulness that challenges corrupt systems and crooked policies, but Jesus didn't flinch from that price. Walter Brueggemann once said that there are two kinds of losers — those who have given up hope and those who don't want things to be any better than they are right now.[6] Those who have given up hope have lost, but often for reasons beyond their control. People who don't want things any better than they are right now know that any change may disrupt the comfortable lifestyles they have built for themselves. Those are the two kinds of losers — those who have given up hope and those who don't want things to be any better than they are right now. Jesus came for the first kind, offering comfort, peace, and hope. Jesus was killed by the second kind.

Jesus talked about his own suffering, but there is some question whether Jesus saw his death as an intentional sacrifice. Especially in the Gospel of Mark, Jesus' prediction of his own demise seems to have more to do with "what the world does to those who follow God's way ... The world does not love you if you question its ways. It may even kill you...."[7] That is not speculation, but a summary of the evidence. Consider those whose lives have been cut short by the assassin's bullet and then ask why.

The Lamb of God has shown us what selfless acts look like, and it is his example that calls us to lose sight of our own lives so that we and all of God's children might know a greater life. We wouldn't expect the call from the Lamb of God to be about anything other than taking up crosses, even when we know that means the death of many things in our lives that we have learned to love. We wouldn't expect the call from the Lamb of God to be about anything other than a painstaking faithfulness that dismisses the popularity we have worked so hard to cultivate over the years. People concerned with remaining popular rarely find time to carry crosses. Dr. King reminded us that we are not fit to live until we have discovered something that we would die for.[8]

All this seems terribly extreme, especially to those of us who have found the church to be one of the few comfortable places left in the world. In fact, this call to risk it all in the making of a better world will not register with most of us. Yet, in the end, the extent to which love is known in the earth and peace reigns on the earth is directly related to the extent to which we open our lives to the possibility that we too have to die to certain things. God works in the lives of all those who allow it, but our hands and hearts are full of things which get in the way. Sometimes we are the ones who resist and oppose the good that God offers. We must die to those things which nurture a divided devotion. We must refuse to keep company with distracting options.

There is a promised land where people live in peace and fairness with one another. Yet, without a willingness to sacrifice, the best we will ever do is see it from a distance.

---

1. Martin Luther King, Jr., April 3, 1968 speech, quoted by Mark Lane and Dick Gregory, *Codename "Zorro": The Murder of Martin Luther King, Jr.* (Englewood Cliffs, New Jersey: Prentice-Hall, Inc., 1977), pp. 116-117.

2. Lane and Gregory, p. 114.

3. John Cartwright, Lecture at Lexington Theological Seminary, Lexington, Kentucky, January, 1996.

4. Leslie Weatherhead, *The Will of God* (Nashville: Abingdon Press, 1944), p. 12.

5. My thanks to Jeff Bell for sharing this personal experience, which I first retold in a sermon published in *Biblical Preaching Journal*, Summer, 1993.

6. Walter Brueggemann, Leslie R. Smith Lectures in *Preaching*, Lexington Theological Seminary, Lexington, Kentucky, April, 1992.

7. Joanna Dewey, "An End to Sacrifice," *Christianity and Crisis*, July 15, 1991, p. 213.

8. Martin Luther King, Jr., quoted in James Cone, *Martin and Malcolm and America: A Dream or A Nightmare* (Maryknoll, New York: Orbis Books, 1991), p. 288.

Essential Personnel!

Matthew 4:12-23

In some parts of the country it doesn't matter, but in many areas the snow which falls during this time of the year can bring things to a decisive halt. Schools close. Events are canceled. Travel becomes tricky. If the conditions become severe enough, the decision may be made that not everybody should try to get to work. Only those who are absolutely necessary should report.

For those occasions we have coined an interesting phrase to describe these people upon whom we depend so much. This phrase sends some people out into the cold to scrape ice off their windshields while others return to the warmth of their beds. This phrase compels some to slip and slide to work at all costs while others do nothing more than watch *Columbo* and *Love Boat* reruns on television.

Even if we live where it rarely snows, the phrase is a familiar one. When budget talks collapse and the government shuts down, this is the phrase that is trotted out. When the earth suddenly moves under the people of California, often a certain group of people are called out while the rest are told to stay at home. When tornadoes blow through the Southwest and disrupt everything in their course, only certain people should risk the dangers involved. These are maintenance people, road crews, ambulance drivers, fire fighters, electric and gas company workers, truck drivers, and a whole host of service people who are taken for granted when things are running smoothly. We call them "essential personnel."

Think about that phrase. Think about what it means to be essential personnel. Then, if you want to be humbled, think about what it is like to be non-essential personnel. Consider the fact that the world can go on without some of us.

The good news is that we are all, or at least all can be, essential personnel. We are called to be a special group of people and to do some important things. In this passage from Matthew, Jesus called some ordinary fishermen to do the work of kingdom-building. Jesus calls ordinary people like you and me to love and serve. And, as in the case of these fishermen, many times we do not need to learn new skills or receive extensive training. Jesus said, "You fishermen have been casting your nets into the sea. Follow me, and you will fish for people." And they did! They were fishermen before, they were fishermen afterwards, but with Jesus the focus and priorities changed.

Jesus says to you and me, "Follow me. You are essential personnel. Come as you are. Bring whatever gifts and talents you have and use them in my name. Bring your excitement and enthusiasm and I will channel them in the right direction. Bring your commitment and I will show you a place where you can make a difference. Bring your love and hope and watch them change lives."

Jesus' disciples were not a panel of experts. Jesus took people whom the world had labeled in many ways non-essential — fishermen, tax collectors, notorious sinners, women who were never considered essential before — and used them and their gifts in doing the work of love and issuing the call to others to follow in the way of Jesus. People who before never felt wanted found a place. People who doubted the world even knew they existed were suddenly essential personnel.

You and I have been made essential personnel, not by our own merit, but because of a "Follow me" we once heard that included us and accepted us and affirmed us. Most of us have heard that voice and those words somewhere along the way. The minister told us she thought we would be good working with the youth. A Sunday school teacher encouraged us to consider ministry. The woman who sits in front of us at church said we would be great in the choir. The church board endorsed our idea to help the needy in the community. Some scripture pointed to an area of our lives in which we could grow in our understanding and service. It happens in many different ways, so do not be surprised if you hear those words, too.

Jesus said, "Follow me," and the exciting thing is that they did. Simon and Andrew, James and John decided to follow Jesus, but they weren't the only ones. All kinds of people responded. Not everybody decided to follow Jesus, but a lot did. From Simon and Andrew to us, women and men, young and aging, people of all colors and classes have heard that invitation in the places where they live their lives.

In fact, Jesus could not stop saying, "Follow me." It is one thing to ask some fishermen to come along for a stroll along the Sea of Galilee, but it is another proposition altogether to utter those words "Follow me" so freely, almost carelessly, that anybody might answer. We know God loves everybody, but just because God loves everybody does not mean everybody is going to follow around after Jesus. Nor does the fact that God loves everybody mean that we want to see all of them in the crowd with Jesus, and with us.

You see, every time Jesus says, "Follow me," it affects us. We don't mind Jesus trying to help the prostitute build some self-esteem, but that doesn't mean we want to be sitting next to her in church. We aren't bothered by Jesus spending time with the mentally ill, but that doesn't translate into our own willingness to be more tolerant of that horrible disease. We are glad to see Jesus healing the sick, those who are on death's door, but that doesn't mean we want the house in our neighborhood converted into a shelter for AIDS patients. We sort of like the idea of Jesus letting children sit in his lap, but that is a long way from appreciating the gifts and presence of children and overlooking the messes created in their celebrations. When Jesus bypasses the church on his way to eat at the house of the most disgusting person in town we are a little miffed, but not nearly as miffed as when Jesus holds that character up as a better model of faith than us.

Suddenly, our excitement over being claimed as essential personnel, people that we would like to think God cannot do without, is tempered by the presence of people who all our lives we have not only shunned, but tried our very best not to be like. Right out in public where people came to draw water, Jesus was seen talking to a Samaritan woman who had been married five times and now was living with another man. Instead of Jesus condemning her, he said, "Here, have a sip of this living water." One day Jesus came upon a woman caught in adultery who was receiving her just punishment. Jesus not only sent the self-appointed jury away, he let the woman go, too. "Neither do I condemn you, so go your way and sin no more." At the most crucial moment Peter denied knowing and following Jesus, so what did Jesus have to say to him later? "Follow me!" And he did!

The temptation is to think that Jesus used exceptional insight when he looked our way and said, "Follow me." It is even a greater temptation to wonder what in the world he was thinking about when he called some of these others, but that is not Jesus' problem. That is our problem, and no explanation on Jesus' part is forthcoming.

In calling these others — in inviting the poor and the lazy and the trash of the earth to the great banquet — Jesus has deemed them essential personnel as well, and some of us are offended by that. Life in the church would be a lot more comfortable if it were just us, but Jesus can't stop saying, "Follow me." Not only can he not stop, he makes this invitation in such an undiscriminating way that most anybody might show up. At a time when churches are knee-deep in marketing techniques that are geared to attract people like those who are already here, Jesus is down by the soup kitchen inviting the homeless family to church. At a time when literature abounds on who we can and cannot expect to come to our church, Jesus insists on knocking on every door in every neighborhood in every section of town. Jesus calls people that we have forgotten about and welcomes people we too often have treated as non-essential, and we are affected every time.

We are affected because the call of God through Jesus is a call away from a divided, fragmented world and into the one family of God where all have a place and all are welcome. It is a call to share a way of life together that the world has said is not reasonable or desirable. Letty Russell, in her book *Church in the Round*, uses a round table as the metaphor for the church. "The round table in itself emphasizes connection, for when we gather around we are connected, in an association or relationship with one another."[1]

When the church is a round table, all are welcome and all have a place. More than that, seating in the round is different from the usual sanctuary arrangement where a pulpit resembles the scene of a lecture, which suggests the truth flows from one person to the rest of the people. At a round table, we gaze upon one another not in judgment or condescension, but in the realization that we need each other's understanding and pieces of the truth in order for our understanding of the truth to be complete.

At the round table we see ourselves in one another. My experience may shed light on your experience. Your way of approaching something may open up new ways of thinking for me. Even in a congregation of predominantly one race and class, which describes most congregations in this country, opportunities abound to learn from the many people who have responded to this invitation of Jesus. Baby-boomers and people born before the Depression can learn from one another. Women and men do not experience the same things in the same ways and from one another can grow in their understanding of themselves and the faith. Older women who never worked outside the home and younger women who must work outside the home have different perspectives and need each other for a balanced view. Ministers and church members do not see things in the same ways and can share thoughts and views as both journey toward the truth.

The opportunities are even greater in churches where urban and rural and people of all classes and colors come to the round table to share in a common life. There is a reason behind Jesus' madness, a reason why he cannot stop saying, "Follow me." It is for our sake. We are not only essential personnel in the work of spreading good news, we are essential personnel for and with one another. We need each other, and there may be no greater grace-filled moment than when we find ourselves sitting at the round table with people we have tried to avoid all these years and learning from them, even as they learn from us.

To you and me, to people of every race and class, to folks of every land and language, indeed, to all of creation, Jesus says, "Follow me." That is not a call to trail along behind Jesus without any intent to share life with one another. It is a call to love as Jesus

75

loved, to welcome as Jesus welcomed, and to take our place alongside our brothers and sisters at the great round table where, for the sake of us all, all God's children are essential personnel.

_____

1. Letty Russell, *Church in the Round* (Louisville: Westminster/John Knox Press, 1993), p. 18.

Blessed Are Those Who Mourn

Matthew 5:1-12

"**Blessed** are those who mourn, for they will be comforted."

In her novel *Come and Go, Molly Snow*, Mary Ann Taylor-Hall gives an account of Carrie attempting to come to grips with the loss of her eight-year-old daughter, Molly Snow. Carrie is a fiddler, but in the wake of this tragic loss she says, "The music doesn't rise up in me right now."[1] In the months that followed, Carrie listens to homespun wisdom and begins the first steps of coming to grips with the absence of Molly Snow and the presence of a deep, dull ache which had taken her place. At one point Carrie remarks, "Sometimes STILL HERE seems stranger than GONE."[2]

Carrie finds it is as hard or harder to deal with being left behind as it is to deal with Molly Snow's being gone. Most anyone who has lost some significant person in his or her life knows that feeling. Without the person we loved, STILL HERE no longer carries the same meaning and joy it once did. When a wife dies, a part of the husband dies, too. When a child dies, a part of the parent dies, too. STILL HERE just isn't the same without them. The plans we made are rendered obsolete. More than that, we wonder how we will go on without the person in whom so much of our lives found their identity and meaning. Stuck in the STILL HERE, Carrie wants to know what is going to happen next. Even as she begins to put her life back together, she admits, "I'm not brave, just cried-out."[3] Finally, Carrie comes to this realization, "I'll always have this grief in the center of me, but my life will grow around it. My life will be real. It will have its moments. It will have music in it."[4]

Blessed are those who mourn, for they will be comforted. We hope so. Carrie isn't the only person ever to have the music stop on her just when it sounded the prettiest. We know what it is like. We have come home and looked in our late husband's chair and expected him to be sitting there. We have wanted to tell a parent about some fantastic achievement in our lives, but had to settle for telling someone else who was not nearly as interested or proud as our parent would have been. We have wanted to call our best friend and talk sports and politics and a hundred other topics that always came up just so we could stay on the line with each other, but no matter how hard we strain we will not hear that voice again.

We know what it is like to mourn. We are not talking about waking up in a bad mood. This is not about a mild disappointment. This is even beyond being sad. We are talking about mourning. When Jacob was given the false report that Joseph had been killed, Jacob put on the uncomfortable garment of sackcloth, which was a sign of hopelessness and despair. When his family tried to comfort him he refused to be comforted (Genesis 37:34). King David was able to move beyond the death of one child (2 Samuel 12:20-23), but the death of Absalom brought weeping and mourning so deep that he could not fulfill his responsibilities. He even cried out that he wished he had died in Absalom's place (2 Samuel 18:31-19:4). When Lazarus died and Jesus was with his sisters and other mourners, Jesus was so moved and disturbed that even he cried (John 11:33-34). In scripture, mourning is characterized by a neglect of appearance, by withdrawing from those close at hand, and by deep, relentless grief.

We recognize it in our own tears and stunned silence and this persistent ache which will not go away. We are talking about mourning, the kind of shaking of the foundations which C. S. Lewis described in *A Grief Observed*. Lewis wrote of his wife after she died of cancer, "Joy's absence is like the sky, spread over everything. There is spread over everything a vague sense of wrongness, of something amiss."[5]

In writing about the Psalms, Walter Brueggemann says that the Psalms are written by and for people who are caught in "the rawness of life."[6] Rather than language that is safe and mundane and socially acceptable, the Psalms employ language that voices our deepest pain. The Psalms are not about denying our losses in the name of keeping things running smoothly. They are concerned instead with people who need to express their anger and grief and heartache. Brueggemann warns against making these Psalms too religious or pious by reminding us that many of them are not courteous or polite. These are the cries of people who have been caught in "the rawness of life." "How long, O Lord? Will you forget me forever? How long will you hide your face from me? How long must I bear pain in my soul, and have sorrow in my heart all day long?" (Psalm 13:1-2). "O Lord, why do you cast me off? Why do you hide your face from me?" (Psalm 88:14). "My God, my God, why have you forsaken me? Why are you so far from helping me, from the words of my groaning? O my God, I cry by day, but you do not answer; and by night, but find no rest" (Psalm 22:1-2).

We know what it is like to mourn, but in this society people who talk the language of the Psalms, people who reveal they are living in the rawness of life, make other people feel uncomfortable. It is much easier to deny the pain than to speak honestly about it.

Perhaps there is value in mourning. Perhaps there is something good that comes out of mourning, even before we get to this promise that those who mourn will be comforted. Rabbi Harold Kushner, in *When Bad Things Happen to Good People*, tells of families asking him if they have to observe *shiva*, which is the memorial week after death when family and friends come to be with those who have lost a loved one. It is similar to visitation at a funeral home or a wake. "Do we really need to sit *shiva*, to have all these people crowding into our home?" they ask. "Couldn't we just ask them to leave us alone?" Kushner writes, "Letting people into your home, into your grief, is exactly what you need now. You need to share with them, to talk to them, to let them comfort you. You need to be reminded that you are still alive, and part of a world of life."[7] Certainly a valuable part of mourning is found in allowing the community of which we are a part to enter our pain and share our loss.

Another reason we should take the time to mourn the loss of a loved one is the way in which it pushes us beyond the denial and into the grief. No one likes to cry, but denying what has happened will hurt us more deeply in the long run than crying. When we mourn we begin to work through our loss. Mourning does not bring instantaneous healing, but it does create a space where healing might happen. A lack of mourning leaves the doors closed to healing and hope. Jesus may have been saying, "Blessed are you who have not given up yet, who continue to live with pain, who keep going even though you miss your loved one more than you can say. Blessed are you who are willing to walk through grief and not around it, for you will be comforted in your honesty."

Still another reason to mourn, especially in those losses which can only be called tragic, is to release our anger. When a person lives a full life, even though it is hard to let go, it does not offend our sensibilities as much as when a young person gets cheated on the seasons. What a horrible thing we have done to healthy anger by looking upon it as a social taboo. We are taught from an early age that polite people control their emotions. More than that, some Christian people were raised with the idea that questioning God is wrong. In scripture, the people who cut loose on God were those who finally were comforted. Something happens when we break down and demand a hearing in the presence of God. It is not a matter of blaming God, though some will. It is not a matter of God's being absent during our greatest need, though some will think that. It is the fact that when we cry out at God, even in anger, all the barriers we have constructed between God and us come tumbling down. In our crying out we are embraced, and in our mourning we are comforted.

A fourth value in mourning is that it gives us the chance to remember. Usually mourning is not a time to make drastic decisions about one's future, but rather a time to reflect and remember and celebrate. These may be the last things we feel like doing, but so many people are moved to thanksgiving when they remember the times spent with their loved one. This is not a ploy to take our minds off the present situation, but an opportunity to recall why the hurt is so deep. It is a chance to consider the difference the person made in our lives, and to recognize that a big part of who we are is wrapped up in this person whom we mourn. Mourning often is painted as a time when all is lost, but this act of remembering calls to mind that not all is lost. We remember the time we spent with the person, both the little incidents that would only mean something to us and the significant events of our lives, and we are reassured that those times can never be taken from us.

Yes, there is value in mourning, but these words from the lips of Jesus promise us more. Jesus promised that those who mourn will be comforted. We just aren't talking about readjusting. We aren't speaking merely of getting by. We are talking about more than simply making it. We are talking about being comforted.

This does not mean we quit crying, or that we no longer miss the person, or that we have somehow gotten over the loss. No, it means quite the opposite. In fact, there are some things we may never get over, but we can learn to live with them. Comfort is not the erasing of a memory, but having our pain soothed to the point that we can remember. Comfort is not a drying of the tears, but a peace that allows us to remember and give thanks even while we cry. The promise of Jesus as he gave his farewell address to the disciples was that God would send to them the Comforter, the Holy Spirit. We too are promised the Comforter, whose constant breath of new life empowers us to continue living in ways that would honor the memory of the one we have lost.

Elizabeth Kubler-Ross described five stages through which a terminally ill patient might pass, though not all of them pass through all of these stages. Those five stages are denial, anger, bargaining, depression, and acceptance. Most families and friends make similar treks, though not all of them reach acceptance either. It is important to note that the stage of acceptance is not a happy time in which all is suddenly okay, but rather a time in which fear and despair no longer wield control over us. Acceptance is not about saying that things worked out fairly well after all, but rather living peacefully and hopefully in the face of a set of completely unsatisfactory circumstances. It is not a giving in to the tragedy, but an overcoming of its grip on us.[8]

Blessed are those who mourn, for they will be comforted. Part of that comfort comes as we openly and honestly mourn the loss of someone we hold dear. Part of that comfort comes through the presence of God's spirit. Part of it surely comes through the gift and power of love. We would not be mourning if we had not loved so deeply. The love which caused the pain to be so great is a love capable of giving us an equal measure of comfort, and therein lies the good news for all who mourn this day.

---

1. Mary Ann Taylor-Hall, *Come and Go, Molly Snow* (New York: W. W. Norton and Company, 1995), p. 18.

2. *Ibid*, p. 120.

3. *Ibid*, p. 219.

4. *Ibid*, p. 268.

5. C. S. Lewis, *A Grief Observed* (New York: The Seabury Press, 1963), p. 11 and p. 40.

6. Walter Brueggemann, *Praying the Psalms* (Winoma, Minnesota: St. Mary's Press, 1986), pp. 17-22.

7. Harold Kushner, *When Bad Things Happen to Good People* (New York: Avon Books, 1981), p. 120.

8. Elizabeth Kubler-Ross, *On Death and Dying* (New York: MacMillan Publishing Company, 1969), pp. 99-106.

How Much Sin Is Too Much?

Matthew 5:13-20

Of all the pressing questions of the day, a sign on one person's desk asks, "How much can I sin and still go to heaven?" The question seems amusing until we stop to think about it. Inherent in this question is a bold-faced confession that there is no interest at all in pursuing a life shaped wholly by the spirit of God, but at the same time we do not want to be so recklessly sacrilegious that we forfeit completely the rewards of the hereafter.

The late Southern humorist Lewis Grizzard said thinking about hell scared the you-know-what out of him. One day he received a questionnaire in the mail titled "Heaven: Are You Eligible?" Grizzard said he took the test and scored "too close to call."[1] How much can I sin and still go to heaven? Lest we fail to recognize the question in that form, perhaps these will sound more familiar. How often can I miss worship and still remain in God's favor? How much prayer time can I forsake and still count on God to hear my prayers when they are the most urgent?

We try to walk the tight rope between doing a lot of things that we want to do for ourselves, but we are careful not to get so carried away that we fail to attend to the things of God. It is a balancing act we attempt in other areas of our lives. Shortly after people learn to drive they discover an interesting twist to the law. While studying for the written part of the examination required to get a driver's license, we find that the rule book makes it quite clear that the speed limit is precisely set. In most places it is 65 miles per hour on limited-access highways. If we ask an officer who administers the written test, she will tell us that the speed limit is 65 miles per hour. However, what we soon learn, through sources we cannot reveal, is that police officers allow drivers anywhere from three to five miles per hour over the speed limit. On most days of the year, 65 miles per hour really means 68 or even seventy miles per hour. The exceptions are holidays. Then 65 really means 65.

While surely none of us participate in such cunning calculation on our roads and highways, some people somewhere probably do. You know how some people are! They read 65 on the signs, but they drive seventy because they can get away with it. The question becomes, "How much can I get away with and not have to pay any consequences or lose any privileges?"

Cosmic judgment is not going to fall on us for driving three or five miles over the speed limit. We probably should not speed. It is not as safe in many cases to speed as it is to drive the speed limit. It may even cost us some serious money in court if we push it too far, but "fudging" on the speed limit will not lock us out of God's family. However, this attitude which puts our speedometers close to seventy miles per hour, which is more than what is allowed but less than what will get us ticketed, has a way of finding its way into a lot of our thinking. It has the ring of, "How much can I sin and still go to heaven.?"

This is an attempt to justify the presence of sin in our lives instead of trying to eliminate it. This is an effort to bargain with God, to renegotiate the terms. Jesus said, "You shall love the Lord your God with all your heart, and with all your soul, and with all your mind, and your neighbor as yourself" (Matthew 22:37, 39). We are simply asking that the requirements be softened a bit. Is it not enough that we make as much room for God in our hearts as we do for the other things we love in our lives? Is it not enough that we pray occasionally, or must we love God with the kind of depth that would require our whole souls? Is it not enough that we know a few favorite verses of scripture, or must we continue to open our minds to the things we either have not heard or are not interested in hearing?

The temptation is to call sin something else, to rationalize that whatever we said did not hurt anybody. It is true that many times what we say and do doesn't hurt anybody else, but it hurts us. Our actions construct a barrier between God and us, regardless of whether anybody else is affected by them. As for the temptation to call sin something else as a way to make it sound okay, that sounds very similar to what the airline industry does in marking their on-time arrivals. A plane can land up to fourteen minutes late and still be considered on-time. Now the question becomes, "How late can I be and still be on-time?" If a plane is four minutes late, it is on-time. If a plane is nine, or ten, or eleven minutes late, it is on-time. "Hey, where you have been. You are twelve minutes late!" "Did you say 'twelve'? Then what is the problem? I am two minutes early!" Just remember, people who come in twenty minutes after their scheduled arrival are in big trouble. They are six minutes late!

The same inclination to call speeding legal, the same temptation to call being late as being on-time, is the same temptation to make some sin acceptable. It is nothing new. When Joseph's brothers finally vented their dislike for their younger brother, the temptation was to kill him. They even made a plan to murder their brother, but then realized it would not profit them any to do so. Instead, they sold him into slavery. The older brothers did not want to kill him, but they wanted him out of their lives. They were tired of Joseph. It would have been a sin to kill Joseph, but it was also a sin to treat him the way they did and sell him as a slave. However, they could get by with that. They probably would not be caught and they could apparently live with themselves, even though this was a terrible thing to do to their brother (Genesis 37:12-28).

The same thing happened in the early church. People were selling their possessions and bringing them to the community so that all would have enough. Ananias and Sapphira sold a piece of property but withheld some of the proceeds. Some of the proceeds he brought to the disciples, but not the entire amount. Ananias must have asked, "What will it hurt if I hold back a little? I am giving a generous amount." Of course, Ananias and Sapphira did not live long enough to ask the question again, "How much can I sin and still go to heaven?" (Acts 5:1-11).

It is not a situation confined to scripture. We ask similar questions. How much can I talk about somebody before it is gossip? How much time can I spend away from the church and still feel connected to its life and worship and service? How long can I ignore the needs of my family and still keep them? How long can I treat my body this way and still expect a long, healthy life?

Sometimes people ask, "How many of the Ten Commandments can I break and still be okay?" These words from Matthew shed a new light on the question. Jesus said, "Whoever breaks one of the least of these commandments, and teaches others to do the same, will be called least in the kingdom of heaven." Just when we thought we were doing fairly well on the Ten Commandments, Jesus throws in all the lesser commandments for us to follow as well. We ask Jesus, "How much sin is too much?" Jesus answers, "Any sin is too much." Not only that, but we get the impression from Jesus' other teachings that maybe we are not even asking the right question.

"How much sin is too much?" Any sin is too much, especially sin that is calculating and intentional. Sin weighs us down. It restricts our freedom. It creates problems in our lives. It makes us live out of fear. It makes us worry about things that are beyond our control. Any sin is too much, and yet we all make mistakes and commit errors and engage in sinful thoughts and words and deeds.

The point is not that we are going to live perfect lives. We are never going to be free of sin, but even to ask, "How much is too much?" is to say we are straddling the fence and holding on for our lives. Even to ask the question says we have one foot in both worlds, wanting to be able to commit to the one but afraid of giving up the other completely. Even to ask the question indicates we are interested in the rewards of the hard and narrow way, but are equally interested in the lifestyle of the wide and easy path.

Elie Wiesel was a teenager when he was taken from his home to the Auschwitz concentration camp. He asked one man there why he prayed and the man replied, "I pray to the God within me that I will be given the strength to ask God the right questions."[2] God gives us the strength, courage, and single-mindedness to ask the right questions. No more are we delving into questions which serve to delay whole-hearted commitment. Now, led in every movement by the spirit of God, we ask different questions. Instead of questions that look for a way out, we ask questions which grow out of loving God with all our hearts, souls, and minds.

As God's spirit shapes our lives, from each thought to each action, questions like this one vanish. We are no longer interested in seeing how much we can get away with. Instead, we awake with a devotion that explores how we can live each day more fully aware of God's guiding presence. We learn to ask new questions.

How can I make choices for God in my work place? How can my personal habits better reflect a sense of God's presence in my life? How can I treat my neighbors in such a way that they feel the love of God through me? How can I free my life of the trappings and clutter in order to live more focused on the ways of God? What new things, O God, are you calling me to learn and do?

Thomas Merton agreed that sometimes we are called not to receive the right answers, but to live the right questions. Merton wrote,

> *My Lord God, I have no idea where I am going ... the fact that I think I am following your will does not mean that I am actually doing so. But I believe that the desire to please you does in fact please you. And I hope I have that desire in all that I am doing. I hope that I will never do anything apart from that desire.*[3]

1. Lewis Grizzard, *A Heapin' Helping of True Grizzard* (New York: Galahad Books, 1991), p. 326.

2. Elie Wiesel, *Night* (New York: Bantam Books, 1960), p. 3.

3. Thomas Merton, *Thoughts in Solitude* (New York: Farrar, Straus and Giroux, 1956), p. 83.

How Long Should We Stay?

Matthew 17:1-9

Mountains were very important to Matthew. When Jesus was tempted to worship the devil in exchange for all the kingdoms of the world, it happened on a mountain. It was good enough for Luke to have Jesus preaching on a nice level place, but when Jesus preaches essentially the same sermon in Matthew he does so on a mountain. That's why we call it the Sermon on the Mount. Jesus went to the mountain to pray. And today we have this story of the transfiguration, which happened on a mountain.

What is it about something happening on a mountain that adds such special significance? For Matthew, whose roots were in the Jewish tradition and who was writing to Jewish Christians, mountains were holy dwellings of God, places where God's presence was known and God's laws were given. Mountains became symbols of the way things would be when God's rule finally would extend over the earth. "Come, let us go up to the mountain of the Lord, to the house of the God of Jacob; that he may teach us his ways and that we may walk in his paths" (Isaiah 2:3).

Whatever we make of this story of the transfiguration, it is no accident that it happened on a mountain. On a mountain the glory of Jesus is revealed and the voice from heaven says, "This is my Son, the Beloved; with him I am well pleased; listen to him!" Who knows what to make of Jesus' face shining like the sun and his clothes becoming dazzling white? And who knows what to make of Moses and Elijah standing there? Who knows what Matthew was trying to tell us with this story? We aren't sure, but we like this idea of mountains.

89

When we are out driving and approach a great stretch of mountains, it is breathtaking and terribly humbling. A drive through the mountains gives us a different perspective on things. Some people invest a lot of time and money in mountain-climbing. That's not for the exercise. They could get the exercise doing a hundred other things. Mountain-climbing is about mastering the mystery and standing where few have stood. We rarely hear of stories about the treacherous descent down a mountain, even though that is great exercise as well. The stories are always about climbing the mountain, risking it all to get to the top, and spending time on some high peak that causes people to see things, and maybe even themselves, differently.

We like the mountains. We even describe some of our greatest moments as mountain-top experiences, but we can't stay on the mountain forever. The emotional level is too intense. However, we can take with us what we experienced on the mountain. A young woman made an announcement one morning to her co-workers, "My honeymoon is over and I am so relieved. Now we can get on with our marriage." That's the way it is with our mountaintop experiences. We can't live there forever. The light is too bright, the pace too frantic, and the demands too great. It is a relief to return to normal lives where we can be ourselves and let others be themselves, but that doesn't mean the honeymoon is forgotten. Just because we don't live on the mountain all the time doesn't mean we forget what happened on the mountain.

One of the most important verses in this reading is verse nine. It begins, "As they were coming down the mountain ..." The mountain-climbing is great, but on Monday people have to go back to work. The honeymoon is great, but then we start to notice the dirty dishes, and the clothes left lying around, and all those annoying habits. We realize we are being led down the mountain and back into other areas of life.

Worship ought to be the closest thing we know on a regular basis to the kind of mountain that was so important to Matthew. Some of these things happen at other times, but worship is that occasion in which the unseen and unknown God is experienced. Here we anticipate some revelation, even if sometimes it is less than earth-shattering. Here we expect some word from the Lord, even if it is a word we have heard many times before. Here some ray of hope ought to lift our spirits and challenge our minds and encourage our best actions.

Maybe it happens in a line of a hymn that we have sung a thousand times, but for some reason it speaks to us this time in fresh ways. It may happen as the words of scripture are read and we hear something that we have never heard before. It may happen when we gather around the Lord's Table and the power of these simple symbols deepens our appreciation for what it means to be followers of Jesus. However it happens, worship ought to be the one place we can count on to experience something of the Sacred.

Now, that's not to say worship services are going to be or are even meant to be what we have come to think of as mountaintop experiences. In fact, some of the things churches are doing to create artificial enthusiasm are disgraceful. Their worship is nothing more than pure entertainment. It is a performance and the congregation is merely invited to sit back and enjoy. Some churches pride themselves on having people in and out of a worship service in 35 minutes. So much effort is given to keeping people interested that little attention is paid to how faithful we are being to the God whom we worship. So many churches are willing to do and be anything in order to attract people that the worship no longer places the demands of God on their lives. Most of these productions lead people into a privatized religion in which worship is geared for each individual. There is no sense of a community of faith and no calling to go out and love the world into a better place.

This is where that critical verse nine comes in. People are drawn to the mountaintop highs. We want things to be interesting. We want to be entertained. In short, we want to stay on the mountain. We fail to see the difference between being entertained and being on the mountain in the biblical sense. In scripture, being on the mountain was about experiencing some revelation, some word from the Lord, some assurance that God was with the people. The mountain had nothing to do with entertainment and everything to do with focusing on what God was doing and on what God was calling the people to do. People who come to worship to be entertained for an hour will surely leave disappointed. People who believe that church ought to be kept interesting regardless of what it takes, surely will leave empty.

Our worship is a matter of our publicly giving thanks to God. The unseen and mysterious God is the focus. In this act of giving thanks, we are shaped into God's people. Something happens here that leads us away from being a collection of individuals and into the formation of a church, a community of faith that lives by certain guiding thoughts and principles. Here we are compelled by the voice from heaven, "This is my Son, listen to him!" Here the truly important things about life and living are revealed to us in ways that we will not hear anywhere else in our culture. Here we come to know the mind of Jesus Christ and begin to appropriate it for our own lives. Here on this mountain we are given a different vantage point, a new perspective from which we can see things that we have missed to this point.

That new vantage point is a must because just when we are about to get comfortable on the mountain, just when we begin to understand some of what is going on, Jesus says, "It's time," and we start back down the mountain. The danger is missing the connection between the time spent on the mountain and the time spent away from the mountain. The temptation is never to associate the sanctuary with the homeless shelter or fellowship hall with the community food pantry. The sin is never to realize that what happens on Sunday is directly related to what happens the rest of the week. And if nothing happens the rest of the week, if there is no tending to the needs of the hurting, no care for the poor, no service done in Jesus' name, then we have made a mockery of what we do on Sunday morning.

In search of any excuse they can find people say, "I can be an equally good Christian outside the church as I can by coming to church." Well, that just isn't so. For one thing, being a Christian assumes being a part of a community. For another, something happens when we worship God together that doesn't happen anywhere else. Here we are molded into the people of God. That's the best reason not to miss church. It's not a matter of "Nice people go to church," or "God is going to get you if you don't go to church."

No, it is the matter of being left behind as the people at worship are formed into a community that lives and believes and acts in the spirit of Jesus Christ. None of us is so far along in the process that we can afford to miss opportunities to grow in our understanding and experience of the faith.

Let's be clear about what we is talking about here. This is not a matter of coming to church for a few moralistic instructions about what to do and not do. Worship is much deeper than that, much more compelling. In worship we express our love for God, and in turn we experience that same love and it shapes us into new people. As we yearn to be heard by God in worship, we are drawn to those in our community who yearn to be heard by us. When we dare to say that our worship is done in the presence of God, we begin to recognize that all of life is lived in that holy presence. Sunday after Sunday, in word, song, and act, we rehearse the story of God's saving grace, and every time we are drawn into it more fully. When we leave it is only natural to see the world and its people through the lens of this grand old story which calls people together in love and peace. We worship in a place full of symbols that point to profound mysteries. When we leave we do so with the reminder that in all of life there is always more going on than we can see with our eyes. In worship we are confronted with a grand vision for the world, and our puny, little horizons are exposed. Something happens when we worship that evokes a response, and that response is lived out daily as we share life in our homes and move about in the community and serve this world that God loves so much.[1]

The key is spending the right amount of time on the mountain. We know we need to be in worship regularly, but if we only worship and never move into the parts of the world that need loving then we have stayed too long. On the other hand, if we don't stay in worship long enough, or fail to immerse ourselves fully in it while we are here, then we will encounter challenges and problems for which we will have inadequate amounts of hope and energy.

The call of Jesus is to go up to the mountain, to experience the Holy One, and to see the world as God wills for it to be. The call of Jesus is also to come down the mountain and into the lives of those who are lonely and oppressed. How long should we stay on the mountain? As long as Jesus tells us to stay. And when should we come back? When Jesus tells us to come back. This is God's son calling, from the mountain and the street corner, from the sanctuary and the soup kitchen; listen to him!

---

1. William H. Willimon, *The Service of God: How Worship and Ethics Are Related* (Nashville: Abingdon Press, 1983)

Books In This Cycle A Series

GOSPEL SET
And Then Came The Angel
Sermons for Advent/Christmas/Epiphany
William B. Kincaid, III

The Lord Is Risen! He Is Risen Indeed! He Really Is!
Sermons For Lent/Easter
Richard L. Sheffield

No Post-Easter Slump
Sermons For Sundays After Pentecost (First Third)
Wayne H. Keller

We Walk By Faith
Sermons For Sundays After Pentecost (Middle Third)
Richard Gribble

Where Gratitude Abounds
Sermons For Sundays After Pentecost (Last Third)
Joseph M. Freeman

FIRST LESSON SET
Between Gloom And Glory
Sermons For Advent/Christmas/Epiphany
R. Glen Miles

Cross, Resurrection, And Ascension
Sermons For Lent/Easter
Richard Gribble

Is Anything Too Wonderful For The Lord?
Sermons For Sundays After Pentecost (First Third)
Leonard W. Mann

The Divine Salvage
Sermons For Sundays After Pentecost (Middle Third)
R. Curtis and Tempe Fussell

When God Says, "Let Me Alone"
Sermons For Sundays After Pentecost (Last Third)
William A. Jones

SECOND LESSON SET
Moving At The Speed Of Light
Sermons For Advent/Christmas/Epiphany
Frank Luchsinger

Love Is Your Disguise
Sermons For Lent/Easter
Frank Luchsinger